Fine WoodWorking

Routers & Router Tables

From the **Editors of** *Fine Woodworking*

The Taunton Press

Text © 2012 by The Taunton Press, Inc.
Photographs © 2012 by The Taunton Press, Inc.
Illustrations © 2012 by The Taunton Press, Inc.
All rights reserved.

The Taunton Press
Inspiration for hands-on living®

THE TAUNTON PRESS, INC.
63 South Main Street, PO Box 5506
Newtown, CT 06470-5506
e-mail: tp@taunton.com

EDITOR: Christina Glennon
COPY EDITOR: Seth Reichgott
INDEXER: Barbara Mortenson
COVER AND INTERIOR DESIGN: Carol Singer
LAYOUT: Susan Lampe-Wilson

Fine Woodworking® is a trademark of The Taunton Press, Inc.,
registered in the U.S. Patent and Trademark Office.

The following names/manufacturers appearing in *Fine Woodworking's Routers
& Router Tables* are trademarks: Amana Tool®, Bench Dog®, Bosch®, Corian®,
DeWalt®, Deft®, Eagle®, Festool®, Grizzly®, Hitachi®, iPod®, Lee Valley®,
Makita®, Masonite®, Porter-Cable®, Ridgid®, Rockler®, Ryobi®, Speed Square®,
Stanley®, Trend®, Triton®, Woodcraft®, Woodpeckers®.

Library of Congress Cataloging-in-Publication Data in progress

ISBN 978-1-60085-759-1

Printed in the United States of America
10 9 8 7 6 5 4 3 2 1

ABOUT YOUR SAFETY: Working wood is inherently dangerous.
Using hand or power tools improperly or ignoring safety practices can lead
to permanent injury or even death. Don't try to perform operations you
learn about here (or elsewhere) unless you're certain they are safe for you.
If something about an operation doesn't feel right, don't do it. Look for
another way. We want you to enjoy the craft, so please keep safety foremost
in your mind whenever you're in the shop.

ACKNOWLEDGMENTS

Special thanks to the authors, editors, art directors, copy editors, and other staff members of *Fine Woodworking* who contributed to the development of the articles in this book.

Contents

Introduction   3

PART ONE

Routers and Bits

- How Many Routers Does Your Shop Need?   **4**
- Trim Routers   **12**
- Heavy-Duty Plunge Routers   **20**
- Ten Essential Router Bits   **28**
- Upgrade Your Router with Shop-Built Bases   **40**

PART TWO

Router Tables

- Router-Table Basics   **50**
- A Versatile Router Table   **62**
- Space-Saving Router Table   **71**
- Rock-Solid Router Table   **78**

PART THREE

Router Jigs and Techniques

- Handheld Routing   **90**
- Essential Jigs for the Router Table   **96**
- Five Smart Router Jigs   **105**
- Versatile Mortising Jig   **113**
- Templates Guide the Way   **116**
- A Guide to Guide Bushings   **122**

- Climb Cutting: Don't Believe the Naysayers **131**
- Eight Tips for Flawless Moldings **138**
- Taper Your Sliding Dovetails for Easier Assembly **148**
- Level Big Slabs in No Time Flat **157**

Metric Equivalents **167**
Contributors **168**
Credits **169**
Index **170**

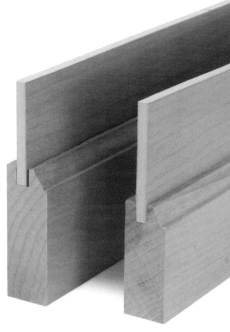

Introduction

At its heart, a router is just a handheld motor that spins a cutting bit, with no built-in way to guide its path. The simplest solution is to use bearing-guided bits, and a lot of woodworkers stop there, making a few moldings and secretly wondering what all the fuss is about. This comprehensive guide will show you why so many woodworkers rave about the router. The secret is controlling its motion. Do that and there is next to nothing the tool can't do. You'll find all of the best approaches here, from the basic edge guide to template guides, smart fences, and the king of all router jigs: the router table. Armed with these, you'll be able to cut perfect joints of all kinds, crank out stacks of matching multiples from a single pattern, level big slabs, and do too many other things to list.

There are lots of ways to make router jigs, and plenty of ink has been spilled on the subject. But this collection of articles is different. All are culled from *Fine Woodworking* magazine, whose editors travel throughout North America to find the most talented and efficient craftsmen out there, people who do incredible work but won't waste their own time or yours building ultimate super-jigs that never pay off. Almost all of these jigs and fixtures are elegantly simple, costing you nothing more than a trip to your scrap pile and an hour or less of time.

You'll get the basics first—how to choose wisely from the dizzying array of routers and bits—before diving into a host of tips and techniques. Plus you'll get four plans for shopmade router tables, helping you find just the right one for your shop. Master this versatile tool and you'll be doing better work in no time, conquering tasks you didn't think were possible, and becoming yet another router fanatic.

—Asa Christiana
Editor, *Fine Woodworking*

How Many Routers Does Your Shop Need?

JEFF MILLER

Doing a quick inventory of my shop recently, I discovered that over the years I have accumulated nine routers. Nine! How did that happen? Does the average woodworker really need that many routers?

The short answer, happily, is no. Still, the argument for having more than one router is powerful. You can leave one in your router table and have another for handheld work.

Second, adding a router with particular strengths can make certain tasks much more convenient, whether you're cutting edge profiles with large, heavy bits or routing shallow hinge mortises on narrow stock.

There are many router types available, but which ones do you really need? I'll suggest two approaches. Either one will tackle a wide range of work, but the first is kinder to your wallet.

Whenever possible, you should do your routing on a table. Moving the workpiece against a solid fence and table is simply more accurate than moving the router.

There are lots of tasks that can't be done on a router table, such as most stopped cuts and cuts in the middle of large surfaces. For those jobs, you'll need a handheld router, and a powerful plunge router will handle them all.

For good value, start with a combo kit

A combination router kit is a very cost-effective way of setting up your shop for both table and handheld routing. The kit comes with one router motor and two bases—one fixed, one plunge. This lets you mount the fixed base in a table and keep the other for topside use.

I recommend putting the fixed base in the table, mainly because the plunge base is

(continued on p. 10)

While you can live without a small "trim" router, the truth is that many routing tasks are light ones, and this compact tool acts like an extension of your arm.

Kill two birds with one combo kit

A combination kit will handle both table and topside routing and costs much less than two separate routers, so you'll have plenty of money left over for a good-quality trim router. Also called laminate trimmers, these small, simple, one-handed routers are easy to set up and even easier to use.

Plunge base

COMBINATION KIT
handles table and handheld routing.

Fixed base

TRIM ROUTER
is great for detail work.

ONE IN THE TABLE

The fixed base lives in the table. Attach the base to the router-table insert (left). Look for a combination kit that offers through-the-table height adjustment (center). The table's flat surface and square fence simplify dozens of tasks, like routing precisely along a narrow edge (right).

ONE THAT CAN PLUNGE

The plunge base is best for handheld routing. The motor switches quickly between the two bases for topside use (above left). The plunge function lets you lower the bit safely into the work while the tool is running. This allows you to make stopped cuts like the dadoes above right and to do them in several passes.

AND ONE IN THE HAND

Hinge mortises and much more. The easily balanced trim router is perfect for this application, which requires delicate control and good visibility. You'll also love it for flush-trimming face frames, inlay work, and when you need to chamfer or round over all the edges on a project.

Stand-alone routers are a heavy-duty upgrade

A router combo kit will cover your table and handheld routing needs, but not as well as two separate routers will. A router designed for table use makes above-the-table bit changes and height adjustments easier and also collects dust efficiently. A dedicated plunge router offers better height and plunge adjustments. And both offer bigger motors for smoother cuts.

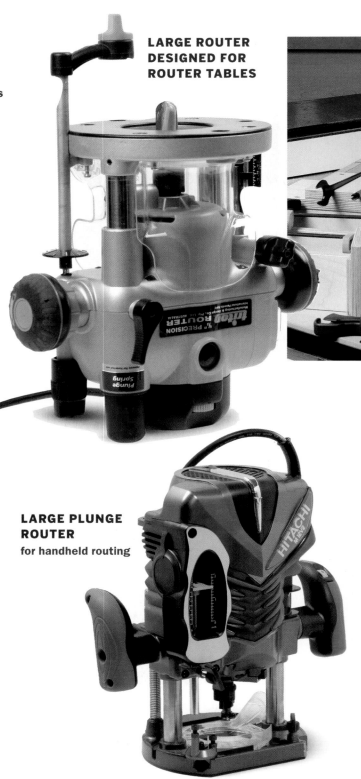

LARGE ROUTER DESIGNED FOR ROUTER TABLES

LARGE PLUNGE ROUTER
for handheld routing

TRIM ROUTER
for detail work

ONE IN THE TABLE

Easy adjustments. This Triton® router includes an automatic spindle lock that makes above-the-table bit changes a breeze.

Bigger bits. In addition to more convenient features, a heavy-duty table router easily removes a lot of stock safely in one pass, as with this panel-raising bit.

One job to do. A dedicated table router stays put, ready for action at a moment's notice.

ONE THAT CAN PLUNGE

Serious power. These maple bed posts require a mortise ½ in. wide and 1¼ in. deep. Tasks like this call for serious routing power, and extra heft helps, too.

There's always room for more

Even with three versatile routers in your shop, there are some situations when it can be nice to have another router or two dedicated to specific tasks. Many woodworkers, especially pros, settle into patterns of work and do certain jobs over and over.

A fixed-base router makes a great fourth router because it's less expensive and very simple to operate. The assembly typically has a low center of gravity and handles easily. The motor also slides into the base in a way that makes depth adjustment simple.

In my case, I often cut edge profiles with larger bits. So I keep a fixed-base router set up with an extra wide base that has a handle to help prevent tipping. I don't use it for anything else.

Or suppose that you regularly cut dovetails with a jig or cut sliding dovetails with an edge guide. You

Add a fixed-base router. An extra router can be dedicated to a single task. Miller keeps an offset base on one of his routers for better balance when molding edges.

might want to have a router set up with a straight bit to clear the waste and another one set up with the dovetail bit to cut the socket.

A router for every router bit? Now that's excessive.

so much more versatile for topside use. Also, when the router is mounted in the table, it's often easier to adjust bit height with the fixed base than it is with the plunge. This makes for an economical choice—you can find a good combination kit for around $200, saving $50 to $100 or more compared with the purchase of two individual routers of a similar size and power.

To the combo kit, add a trim router. Although its limited horsepower confines it to lighter-duty tasks, it is much easier to control than a larger router. It is also limited to working with ¼-in.-shank bits, but its

lower torque and one-handed size are perfect for hinge mortising, inlay, and small edge profiles like chamfers and roundovers. It's great for any task that doesn't call for large bits, deep cuts, or lots of horsepower.

With this package of routers, you can tackle almost everything.

Stepping up

The combination kit is a great value, but it does force a few compromises. For one, switching one motor between table and topside is much less convenient than having two individual routers. Second, in most

If one is good, two are better. You will simplify tasks that require two bits, like sliding dovetails, by using a pair of routers. In this setup, with the router base riding a fence, the routers should be identical.

combination kits the motor is limited to 2 hp or 2¼ hp. If you cut deep mortises with your router or work with large shaping or panel-raising bits, you should consider investing in more horsepower (see p. 8). A heavy-duty plunge router will typically come with better features than the plunge base in a combo kit. You'll get height adjustment that is easier and more accurate, a smoother plunge mechanism, and a handle-mounted power switch. Also, the 3¼-hp motor will provide smooth, effortless action on the heaviest cuts.

As another step up from the combination-kit approach, I'd recommend getting a router built to be installed in a table. Routers of this type come with a through-the-table lift. This lets your router table become a dedicated shop tool with excellent controls, like a tablesaw, instead of something you have to fuss with for 15 minutes just so you can spend 30 seconds cutting an edge.

Again, add a trim router to this combination and you're set to tackle the full range of routing tasks.

Trim
Routers

GREGORY PAOLINI

In the past, trim routers were tools designed for a single carpentry task: trimming countertop laminate. Recently, however, manufacturers have responded to user feedback with features that make these tools more versatile and easier to use. The best routers in this new crop are perfectly suited to a variety of furniture-making tasks: rounding over and chamfering edges, routing hinge mortises, flush-trimming veneer and edgebanding, routing cavities for inlay, and more. Their small size and light weight makes them agile, so they are easy to move around corners and along curves, and to balance on edges and narrow parts like legs. And they can be used one-handed, which means you can fly around a workpiece, holding the router and easing the edges with one hand while holding and repositioning the workpiece with the other.

There are a lot of new models on the market, and choosing one is difficult if you can't get them all in the shop and try them out. But I've done just that, so you don't have to. I gathered 12 compact routers in my shop and used them daily as I made furniture. Over the course of several months, clear winners emerged.

Put to the furniture-maker's test

There are a lot of empirical measurements—such as spindle runout—that can be taken when testing a router. But what ultimately

Much more than a laminate trimmer. No longer just a countertop installer's tool, today's trim routers excel at a variety of woodworking tasks. From routing mortises for hinges and inlay to rounding over edges and trimming edgebanding flush, the best new routers offer the perfect combination of power, precision, and control.

Inlay

Hinges

Banding

Edges

Bit height should be easy to adjust. Trim routers are used for small work, where a bit that is a few thousandths of an inch too deep can spell disaster. Bit-height changes should be uncomplicated and accurate. The Ridgid's® thumbwheel system was the best.

Simpler design gets the job done. The lead screw on the Makita® (above) and Grizzly® H7791 controls all bit-height adjustments.

The twist is good, too. When using the fixed base on the Porter-Cable® 450PK (above) and its close relative, the DeWalt® 611PK, all height adjustments are made by releasing a locking lever and then turning the motor in the base, another system that works very well.

Two that are less precise. Bit adjustments on the Ryobi® (left) and Grizzly H7790 are similar. Release the lock and then push and pull the motor until you get the height you want. That's OK for coarse adjustments, but it's a struggle for fine changes.

A clear view makes for easier routing. When routing mortises for inlay or hinges, you need to stay within the layout lines, so visibility is key. A base with a large cutout and clear sub-base, like the DeWalt's, creates the perfect window, letting you see exactly what you're routing.

Tunnel vision. The base on the Porter-Cable 7301 offers a great view of the bit up high, but the sub-base is opaque and has a small opening, so it is very difficult to see what the bit is routing.

matters is power, cut quality, how easy the router is to use, and how comfortable it is to hold while you're using it.

So I skipped the measurements, took the routers out to the shop, and used them the way a furniture maker would. To gauge cut quality, I rounded over and chamfered furniture edges. Then I routed hinge mortises and cavities for inlay. After the formal tests, I used all of them as I went about my daily work. As I used them, I took note of whether they ever bogged down due to a lack of power.

To keep a level playing field, I equipped each router with new Whiteside router bits, chosen because they have performed well in previous *Fine Woodworking* magazine tests. However, for flush-trimming edgebanding,

the Festool® needed a proprietary bit, which the manufacturer provided. But this had no effect on my overall impression of the router.

Here's what I discovered. Power is not a problem and neither is cut quality. All of these routers did everything I asked of them without a problem and left a clean, chatter-free surface. But there was a difference when it came to usability and comfort. The DeWalt DWP611PK was the easiest to use and the most versatile, so it is my pick for best overall. For best value, I picked two routers. The Ridgid R2401 has fast, precise height adjustments, an LED light for improved visibility, and is great for one-handed use. Because of its low cost, the Grizzly H7791 is the perfect choice for a router that you leave set up for one task.

Trim routers head to head

DEWALT 611PK

This revolutionary new tool is a smaller version of the popular two-base router kits. It's compact like a trim router, but more powerful. Both bases are well-designed. The fixed base has excellent height adjustments, is comfortable for one-handed use, and has a rough exterior that provides a solid but comfortable grip. An elongated, square sub-base improves the router's balance on narrow parts and rides easily against a straightedge. The plunge base is just as good. Its small size is ideal for inlay work. Both bases offer great visibility, too. And there is an LED light built into the motor housing that makes more precise work much easier.

BEST OVERALL AUTHOR'S CHOICE

www.dewalt.com
Amps: 7
Weight: 4 lb. (fixed);
6.6 lb. (plunge)

www.grizzly.com
Amps: 1.7
Weight: 3.6 lb.

GRIZZLY H7791

BEST VALUE AUTHOR'S CHOICE

The Grizzly lacks LED lighting and variable speed, and height adjustments are more difficult than on the DeWalt 611PK and Ridgid R2401. Also, it is not as comfortable as those two routers, but with its low price, it is a great choice for a router dedicated to one job, like rounding over edges. Then you can lock it in place and leave it alone. Always at the ready, this router will save you time and effort. It is also light and easy to hold, perfect for one-handed use as you race around the edge of a tabletop. I am tempted to buy two or three, setting up each one for a different task.

RIDGID R2401

I loved using this elegantly simple trim router because bit-height adjustments are quick and accurate. There is a lead screw for micro-adjustments, but a push of your thumb disengages the mechanism so that rough adjustments can be made. It also is comfortable to hold, making it a favorite when it came time to round edges. There's a large opening in the base, a clear sub-base, and an LED light, all of which add up to great visibility. Bit changes are a snap. There also is a second, square sub-base, which is just what you need to guide the router with a straightedge, and an edge guide. It can't match the DeWalt's versatility, but it is easier to handle for light routing and much less expensive.

BEST VALUE AUTHOR'S CHOICE

www.ridgid.com
Amps: 5.5
Weight: 3.8 lb.

www.boschtools.com
Amps: 5.6
Weight: 3.8 lb.

BOSCH® COLT

The Bosch is comfortable to hold. It also is bottom-heavy, so it was well-balanced and stable in use. The square base works well with a straightedge, and bit-height adjustments are quick and easy. But it does lack LED lighting, and the black sub-base limits visibility.

www.dewalt.com
Amps: 5.6
Weight: 3.6 lb.

DEWALT 26670

I've done a lot of laminate work, and this router would be a workhorse for trimming laminate flush to countertops and profiling edges. However, the sub-base is opaque and limits visibility, so tasks like mortising for hinges and removing material for inlays—two important and frequent tasks in furniture making—are difficult at best.

www.festoolusa.com
Amps: 6
Weight: 5.2 lb.

FESTOOL MFK 700

I tested this router with two bases. One held it vertically, but in that configuration the bit is completely hidden by the base and it was not easy to hold in one hand. Those are serious problems for a furniture maker. The second base holds it horizontally, which turned it into the best tool I have ever used for trimming edgebanding flush.

www.grizzly.com
Amps: 2.1
Weight: 3.8 lb.

GRIZZLY H7790

This router has a clear plastic base and sub-base, so visibility was great. However, the motor is both heavy and top-heavy, so the balance wasn't good. And adjusting the bit height is somewhat tricky. After the locking lever is released, the motor rotates and slides in and out freely. Setting the height involves a fair amount of trial and error.

www.makita.com
Amps: 4
Weight: 3.6 lb.

MAKITA 3709

A rack-and-pinion system makes fine and coarse adjustments easy. The power cord comes out of the top, improving the balance. But this wasn't a comfortable router: the housing didn't fit my hand well, and the edge-guide locking knob was often in the way.

Trim routers head to head (continued)

www.portercable.com
Amps: 7
Weight: 4 lb. (fixed);
6.6 lb. (plunge)

PORTER-CABLE 450PK
The Porter-Cable 450 is almost identical to the DeWalt 611PK. But the differences are where it falls short. There are no LED lights, so visibility isn't as good. Also, the body of the fixed base has painted ridges running parallel to your fingers, resulting in a slick surface. And the sub-base is round, so it's not as good for use with a straightedge.

www.portercable.com
Amps: 5.6
Weight: 3.8 lb.

PORTER-CABLE 7310
This Porter-Cable is practically a twin of the DeWalt 26670. Other than a few cosmetic differences, they differ only in that the Porter-Cable's adjustment knob is not as nice as the DeWalt's and the Porter-Cable is flat on top, rather than domed. In terms of performance, they are practically identical.

www.ryobitools.com
Amps: 4.5
Weight: 6 lb.

RYOBI TR45K
The Ryobi fit well in my hand and was comfortable to use for extended periods of edge-chamfering. However, it was difficult to set the bit height, because the motor slides freely in the base. Height is adjusted by pushing the motor in or pulling it out, an approach that works for coarse changes but makes fine adjustments difficult.

www.trend-uk.com
Amps: 6.6
Weight: 6 lb.

TREND® T4
This is a dedicated plunge router. It worked great for inlay work and routing hinge mortises. However, it is just as large as my mid-size plunge routers. That means it isn't well-suited for one-handed work like rounding over or chamfering edges. Also, the fit and finish were a bit rough, with a few burrs here and there.

Unique features to consider

A new angle on flush-trimming. Festool's horizontal base turns the motor 90° and provides a stable platform for trimming edgebanding—a huge improvement over balancing a router on the thin edge.

Plunge bases are perfect for inlay. Tipping a fixed base into a mortise can be tricky, so if you do a lot of inlay work, consider the Trend T4 (a dedicated plunge router), the DeWalt 611PK, and the Porter-Cable 450PK.

Heavy-Duty Plunge Routers

GREGORY PAOLINI

Whenever practical, I rout my mortises, and there's no better router for the job than a plunge router with a big motor. The raw power lets you remove more waste in a single pass, and the increased mass means the router is easier to control and cuts more smoothly. But a big plunge router is great for more than just mortises. I use mine for template routing, profiling edges, and cutting dadoes and rabbets. That's why I was glad to say yes when I was asked to test all the heavy-duty plunge routers on the market.

Three-up routers make deeper cuts than mid-sized models and feel more solid in your hands.

The things you do most should be easy to do. Bit changes are easiest on the Triton. The spindle locks automatically, which frees up one hand to hold the router body for more stability.

Trigger switches are convenient and safe. Both hands grasp the router when it starts. Festool, Bosch, and Porter-Cable routers all have one.

Two smart ways to adjust speed. With Hitachi's thumbwheel (left), both hands stay on the handles during speed changes. The Porter-Cable marks speed with RPM (right), so it can be set exactly to a bit's required speed.

It takes a lot of power to breeze through deep mortises, so I looked only at routers with 3-hp motors. That's a lot of torque and power to have between your hands, so the routers needed a soft start to tame torque at startup and variable speed so that the motor can be slowed down for large-diameter bits.

Also, I wanted all of the routers to work with guide bushings, making them more flexible for template routing than if you had to rely on bearing-guided bits. Fixed-base routers weren't considered because they aren't suited for routing mortises. In the end, I tested seven plunge routers: the Bosch 1619EVS, DeWalt DW625, Festool OF2200, Hitachi® M12V2, Makita RP2301FC, Porter-Cable 7539, and Triton TRC001.

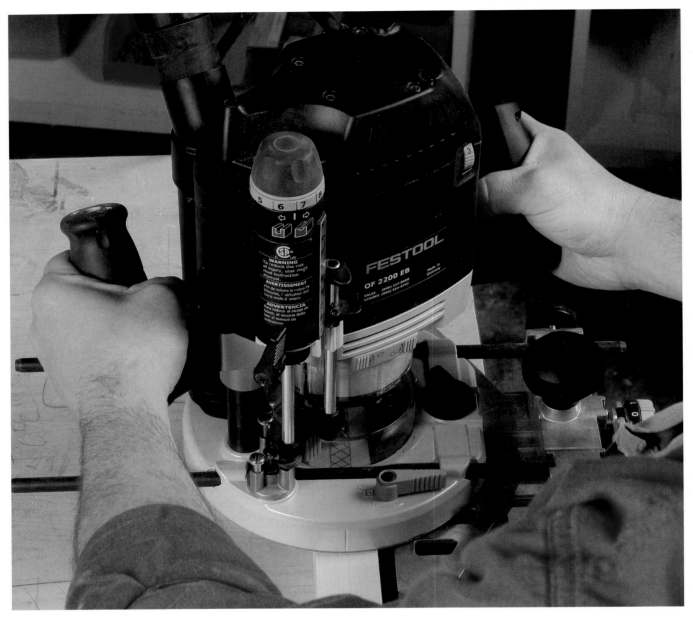

Festool puts your hands at a comfortable angle. That means your wrists are straight. Not only is this more comfortable, but it also gives you more control.

Power and cut were not an issue

The primary reason to use a powerful 3-hp plunge router is to hog away waste more quickly. But all of that power is worthless if the cut ends up burned or bumpy. To get a sense of the power in these routers, I routed mortises in hard maple. To test cut quality, I routed two edge profiles (a roundover and an ogee) in cherry, which is prone to burning. To ensure that I was testing routers and not router bits, I equipped every router with its own set of new Whiteside router bits, which have been top performers in previous tests.

All of the routers had enough power to rout the mortises with ease. I even used them to rout mortises 1 in. deep by ½ in. wide by 3 in. long in one pass. Cut quality wasn't a problem either. Every router left behind a surface free of chatter and burning on the edge profiles, which I also cut in a single pass.

It comes down to ease of use, comfort

The increased power of big plunge routers comes at a price. They also are heavier, and if that mass isn't easy to control, the router won't be easy to use. I took note of how comfortable the handles were, how easy it was to reach and use the power switch and plunge lock, and how smoothly the router plunged and came back up in all situations.

I also spent time doing basic router tasks like changing bits, adjusting bit height, and adjusting the height of the turret stops. If any of these tasks are a pain, you will quickly tire of using the router.

The routers' edge guides and guide-bushing systems also got a close look. A problem with either one causes frustration and costs time, money, and material. I also evaluated each router's dust collection, because without effective dust collection, a router is a messy tool. As it turned out, dust collection is a problem for all of the routers except the Festool.

Considering all of these factors, one router stood out: the Festool OF2200. It's my choice for best overall. Ergonomically, it was the most comfortable router to use. Dust collection is excellent. The guide fence is the best of the bunch, with a great micro-adjustment knob. On the downside, the Festool's scale is metric only. I don't mind that, but I know others will.

However, the Festool OF2200 isn't for everyone. The router is expensive. It will cost even more to add the accessory kit that includes the edge guide and guide-bushing

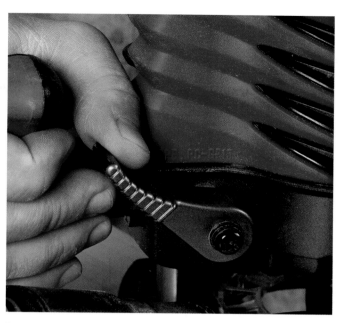

Levers control plunge on most routers. The best ones, like on the Hitachi, can be reached without letting go of the handle, and require little force.

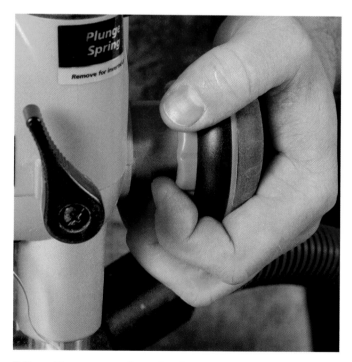

Triton offers a second way to plunge. Pull in the orange lock collar and twist the handle to lower the body on a rack-and-pinion gear. It's a nice way to get precise plunge control.

Adjustable plunge stops are more versatile than preset ones. They give precise control over how much material is removed on each pass. All but the Bosch have them.

Height adjustments are easy on the Bosch. Loosen the lock and twist the knob. The depth rod raises and lowers on a rack-and-pinion gear.

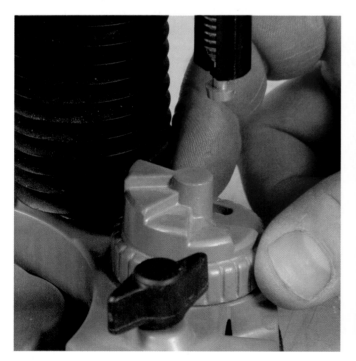

Bosch's turret has preset stops. There is a ⅛-in. difference between the six stops. This saves setup time but can be a bother if your plunge depth isn't a multiple of ⅛ in.

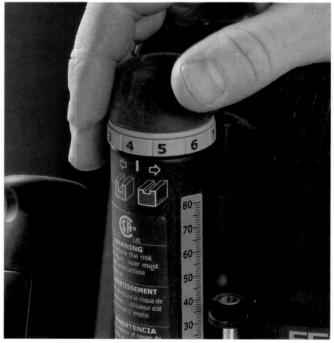

Festool offers very fine micro-adjustments. The numbered and audible detents on the knob are separated by 0.1 mm.

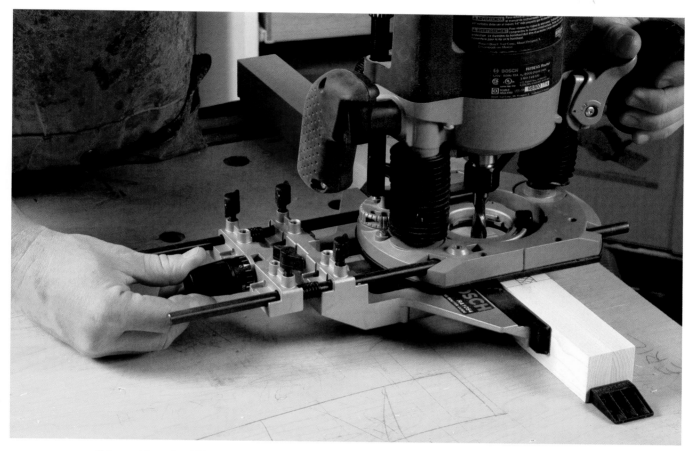

Edge guides should have fine adjustment. All but the Triton offer micro-adjusters. After rough setting the guide and taking a test cut, you can dial in the perfect distance.

system. That led me to think about which router I would pick if I excluded the Festool from consideration. Again, the choice was obvious. The strangely futuristic-looking Hitachi M12V2 is a great router. It handles well, plunges smoothly, and has simple micro and macro height adjustments. Its edge guide (included) is very good, and the router comes with a proprietary guide bushing (none of the other routers come with a bushing) and an adapter for Porter-Cable-style bushings. I have only one gripe about the Hitachi. Its dust collection doesn't work.

Festool's micro-adjust knob is even better. The fence is captured on the screw so that it moves both in and out with adjustments, and the knob is graduated.

Heavy-duty plunge routers

www.festoolusa.com
Weight: 17 lb. 4 oz.

www.boschtools.com
Weight: 13 lb. 4 oz.

BOSCH 1619EVS

At first, this router was uncomfortable, as the plunge-locking lever dug into my wrist. But after repositioning the lever, which required removing it first, I found it comfortable. All of the control buttons and knobs are well-placed and intuitive to use. The router handles very well and plunges smoothly, and the plunge lock works great, holding heights without budging. The add-on accessory edge guide is second only to the Festool's. Bosch's proprietary bushings work fine. A baseplate adapter is supplied with the router, but the bushings are not. The spindle lock worked well and bit changes were easy. A nice drop-forged wrench is supplied with the router. The dust-collection attachment works well, but makes bit changes difficult.

FESTOOL OF2200

The excellent angled grips on this router ensure that your wrists remain straight, which leads to greater control. The dust collection is far and away the best of the bunch. It left just a few chips in the mortises I routed, and it was flawless when routing edge profiles. The Festool also has the smoothest plunge, the best plunge lock, and easy micro and macro height adjustments. The edge guide is superb, and the ratcheting spindle lock works very well. Finally, it was one of only two routers that have an automatic spindle brake, a nice extra when you have a lot of stopping and starting to do. On the down side, the drop-down dust shroud can make it hard to see the bit on deeper plunges. Also, the accessory kit that contains the edge guide and guide bushing system adds to an already lofty price.

HITACHI M12V2

This router plunges smoothly and handles very well. A good edge guide, a proprietary guide bushing, and an adapter for Porter-Cable bushings are standard, which is great given its cost. Adjustments to plunge depth settings are easy, and switching between macro and micro adjustments is simple. You need only flip a well-placed lever. The plunge scale is easy to read. A dial to adjust the motor's speed is embedded in the right handle, right where your thumb can make quick adjustments. On the down side, the router's dust collection is ineffective (as it is on most of the other routers). The spindle lock worked fine, but the wrench is stamped from thin steel and uncomfortable to use.

www.hitachipowertools.com
Weight: 15 lb. 4 oz.

www.dewalt.com
Weight: 13 lb. 6 oz.

DEWALT DW625

With good balance and ergonomics, this router handled well. I especially liked its slick phenolic baseplate, which made it easy to steer the router for edge profiling. It plunges smoothly, and the locking lever works easily and holds the height tightly. The stops on the turret are simple to adjust to allow for variable plunge steps. Adjustments to the plunge depth, both macro and micro, are easy. Bit changes presented no problems, as the spindle lock worked and the wrench was beefy and drop-forged. The dust collection worked very well when I was mortising, but not so well while I was edge profiling. Unfortunately, the edge guide was disappointing, as its fence casting wasn't straight. And visibility became an issue on deep plunge cuts.

www.makita.com
Weight: 13 lb. 12 oz.

MAKITA RP2301FC

With lights in its base, this router had great overall visibility and sight lines. I also appreciated the very aggressive spindle brake, as it minimized the time wasted between mortises. The plunge lock worked well, and the depth rod and turret system were easy to adjust. However, the plunge mechanism was weak, and I occasionally had to help the router back up. The power switch was a nuisance, too. To turn the router on, you must first depress a lockout switch meant to prevent accidental starts. If you don't immediately release the safety switch, the router is locked on and turning it off can be a nuisance.

www.portercable.com
Weight: 17 lb. 4 oz.

PORTER-CABLE 7539

All of the adjustments are easy to make on this router. Motor speed is changed with a slider on top of the motor. It has a trigger switch on the handle, and the turret system is easy to zero and adjust. The baseplate opening is sized for Porter-Cable guide bushings, which is nice. However, it also means that you have to replace the baseplate to use profile bits with a diameter larger than the opening. The optional edge guide is sturdy, but the weight of the long aluminum extrusion sometimes pulled the router off plumb. The optional dust-collection baseplate works well, but we had trouble finding one to buy. There is no spindle lock.

www.tritontools.com
Weight: 13 lb. 14 oz.

TRITON TRC001

Although this router has a standard plunge lever, you can also rotate one of the handles to raise and lower the body with a rack and pinion. The more I used it, the more I liked that option. The round handles are very comfortable. And bit changes were the easiest by far on this router, because the spindle is self-locking. The dust-collection setup looks impressive, but it is overpowered by the motor cooling fan, which sends dust and chips all over. The edge guide is actually an alternate baseplate, which is unique, but it did not glide easily over wood. Also, this is a top-heavy router, which made mortising tricky.

Ten Essential Router Bits

GARY ROGOWSKI

You've bought a new router, unpacked it, and even found the switch on it. But that's only half the battle. Woodworkers new to the router will encounter a bewildering array of bits that do all sorts of work. Which ones do you buy first?

High-quality router bits are not cheap, and making the wrong choices can hurt your wallet and limit your woodworking. So I've come up with a basic set of bits that will do a lot of things well, from cutting joinery to shaping profiles to pattern-routing. The entire kit is well worth the money when you consider all the jobs you can complete with it.

Most of the bits in this group are carbide-tipped, which makes them more durable than high-speed steel bits but less

A BASIC BIT KIT

- ¼-in. straight bit
- ½-in. straight bit
- ⅜-in. spiral-fluted straight bit
- Rabbeting bit with four bearings
- ½-in. dovetail bit
- ¼-in. roundover bit
- ⅜-in.-radius cove bit
- 45° chamfer bit
- Three-wing slot cutter
- ½-in. flush-trimming bit

expensive than solid carbide bits. Also, most have ½-in. shanks, which are less prone to breaking than bits with ¼-in. shanks. I don't claim that these bits will be the only ones you'll ever need, but they will create a rock-solid, versatile foundation for routing that can be expanded as your woodworking repertoire expands.

Operating: Handheld vs. table mounted

For safety, Rogowski does most of his routing on a table because it provides a stable work surface. He uses a handheld router when a workpiece is too unwieldy to handle on a table or when the task simply is more suited to handheld routing, such as chopping mortises or running dadoes across a case side. When using a handheld router, work left to right. When routing on a table, work right to left.

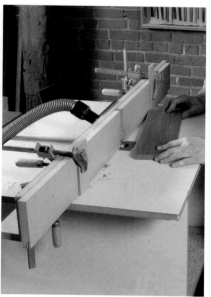

Straight bits

Straight bits do the yeoman's work in a router-bit kit. Designed for square, uniform cuts such as grooves and dadoes, they also can be used to clean up edges and to cut mortises, tenons, and rabbets. Straight bits have straight or spiral flutes. Two useful sizes of straight-fluted bits are ¼ in. and ½ in. (Choose a ¼-in. shank for the ¼-in. bit; a ½-in. shank will limit the depth of cut.) A ⅜-in.-dia. spiral-fluted up-cutting bit is perfect for chopping mortises.

Grooves and dadoes

A groove is cut along the long grain of a board, whereas a dado is cut across the grain. A sharp straight bit makes quick work of both tasks and gives you grooves and dadoes of uniform size.

Generally, grooves are easier to cut on a router table, but it's possible to cut them with

a handheld router. Use a plunge router for stopped grooves. For accuracy, you'll need to employ the router's edge guide or secure a straightedge to the workpiece to guide the router.

Dadoes often are cut in multiples and on longer, wider stock for case goods, so it makes sense to cut them with a handheld router. For speed and accuracy, it's a good idea to use a right-angle jig that clamps to the workbench and across the stock (see the photos below). Fed properly, the router base will be pushed by the cutting action against the fence of the jig, ensuring a straight cut.

Make the jig out of ¾-in.-thick plywood. Screw a fence to the base (both about 4 in. wide) at a precise 90° angle. Place the router base against the fence, then rout a dado in the base of the jig. Use that dado to align the jig with layout lines on the workpiece.

Grooves are best cut on the router table. For smooth cuts with little burning, take light passes, gradually raising the bit to full height.

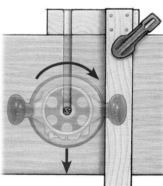

Work on this side of the fence. Then the bit's rotation will pull the router base against the jig's fence, ensuring an accurate cut.

Right-angle jig ensures straight dadoes. Align the dado in the jig with the layout lines on the workpiece, then clamp the jig in place.

Router as jointer

With the help of a jig, you can clean up roughsawn edges on large workpieces such as tabletops. Work from left to right.

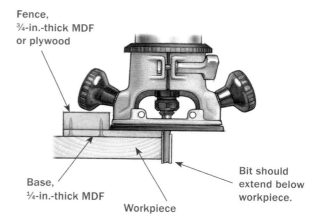

Fence,
¾-in.-thick MDF
or plywood

Base,
¼-in.-thick MDF

Workpiece

Bit should
extend below
workpiece.

Edge trimming

You can use straight bits to make edge cuts just like a jointer. I often use this technique on workpieces such as tabletops that are too unwieldy to clean up on a jointer.

To ensure a straight cut, make a jig a bit longer than the longest edge you need to rout. The jig should have a base of ¼-in.-thick medium-density fiberboard (MDF) and a ¾-in.-thick fence (see the drawing above). Start by using the router to trim the edge of the base. Then just place that edge on the line you want to cut. Be sure the cutting edge of the bit is long enough to reach past the bottom of the workpiece.

Mortises in a flash. Mounted in a plunge router, a spiral bit cuts a mortise easily. Use a router fence for accuracy. To prevent the router base from wobbling on narrow stock, support it with an extra piece of stock.

Use a spiral bit for mortising

It's tough to find carbide-tipped spiral bits these days, so I chose a solid carbide bit for the kit. It's an expensive piece of tooling, but if you plan to cut mortises with a router, this is the bit to have. The flutes spiral around the bit, similar to the way a drill bit is cut, so it pulls chips up and out of the mortise. And with spiral flutes, there are always two cutting edges in the work, making for a smooth, shearing cut.

Rabbeting bit

As the name implies, a bearing-guided rabbeting bit excels at cutting rabbets of varying sizes. Although a straight bit can do the job, the bearing-guided bit ensures uniformity, an advantage if you're cutting a number of identical rabbets.

TIP Don't toss your loose bits in a drawer. If they roll around and bump into each other, the cutting edges could get chipped. Instead, hold bits in their original packaging, or drill a wood scrap to make a simple holder for the set.

A rabbeting bit with a set of different-diameter bearings allows you to change the width of the rabbet simply by switching out the bearings. Rabbets typically are not much deeper than ½ in., so the set I recommend adjusts to cut rabbets from ⁵⁄₁₆ in. to ½ in. wide. You can use the bit in a router table or in a handheld router.

Rabbets made easy. A bearing-guided rabbeting bit allows you to rabbet a glued-up picture frame. You can dial in the depth of the rabbet and prevent tearout by making a series of shallow passes (⅟₃₂ in. to ⅟₁₆ in. deep) until you reach the final depth. You'll have to clean up the corners with a chisel.

Profiling the edges of a frame

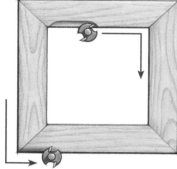

To rabbet the inside edge of a picture frame, move the router clockwise.

To rout a profile on the outside edge, move the router counterclockwise.

One advantage of a bearing-guided rabbeting bit is that you can cut rabbets in frames after they have been glued together, which ensures perfect alignment. The bearing controls the rabbet's width, so there's no need for a fence to guide the cut. Move the router clockwise around the inside of the frame (see the drawing above right).

TIP Buy quality bits from reputable sources. Generally, a cheap bit won't last as long as its pricier cousin because it's not as well made. You could end up spending twice as much to replace a bit that dulls prematurely, breaks, or chips.

Three-wing slot cutter, 1/4 in. thick

A slot cutter makes grooves to a specific, consistent depth and width with a cleaner cutting action than a straight bit. It is used mainly for cutting grooves for a frame-and-panel assembly, but it also can be used to rabbet the edges of panels and to carve decorative grooves in panels or pilasters. Each of these jobs is best done on a router table.

I chose a bit with three wings that cuts a 1/4-in. kerf. Three wings provide more balance than two. The smaller kerf allows you to cut grooves for 1/4-in.-thick panels as well as larger ones with a series of passes. You can change the depth of cut by changing the bearing.

1/2-inch dovetail bit

Dovetail bits are designed to make dovetails for drawers or carcases as well as sliding dovetails. Most dovetail bits have angles ranging from 7° to 14°. I prefer the 10° angle, which works well for both hard and soft woods.

Both parts of a sliding dovetail joint can be cut on a router table. Dovetail bits are made to cut full depth. So before you cut a sliding dovetail slot, run a 1/4-in. straight bit through first to clean out most of the waste. Follow with the dovetail bit. This will extend the life of the bit and leave a cleaner cut.

Cut the slot first, with the stock held flat on the table and a backer board behind it to keep the workpiece square to the fence and prevent blowout. With the bit height unchanged, reset the fence to cut the dovetail on the end of the mating piece. Make test cuts in a scrap piece the same thickness as the stock.

Sliding dovetail: Solid and sturdy. Make the slot first, holding the board flat on the table (above left). Leave the height of the bit as is, and adjust the fence to cut the mating dovetail with the stock held vertically against the fence (above right). Again, use a backer board to prevent tearout and to keep the workpiece aligned.

45° chamfer bit

The chamfer bit is used to bevel the edge of a workpiece. The 45° model I've included in this kit (1¼ in. dia.) is the most common. It's faster than a block plane for creating uniform chamfers on legs, aprons, and tabletops. You also can use it to achieve great visual effects (see the photo below). The bearing on the bottom of the bit allows you to make cuts without a fence. To increase the depth of the chamfer, raise the bit.

Eased edges. A 45° chamfer bit can soften the edges of legs, aprons, and tabletops.

Thick and thin. You can make a beefy top look thinner by chamfering the bottom edge and a thin top look thicker by chamfering the top edge.

Roundover and cove bits create a classic profile

You can combine roundover and cove bits to create an ogee profile with a fillet. Make the first pass with the cove bit, then finish with the roundover cutting full depth.

FIRST ROUT THE COVE

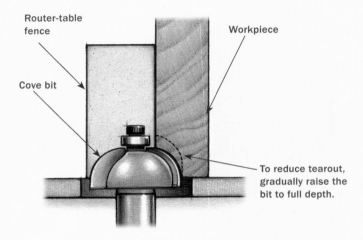

Router-table fence

Cove bit

Workpiece

To reduce tearout, gradually raise the bit to full depth.

THEN SHAPE THE ROUNDOVER

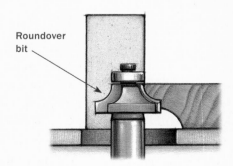

Roundover bit

Two profiles, one bit. Use the roundover bit to create a soft edge (bottom) or a rounded edge with a step, or fillet, along the top of the profile.

¼-inch roundover bit

A bearing-guided roundover bit eases sharp corners and softens the look of a piece. The ¼-in. bit is a good moderate size to start your collection, because it will cut roundovers with or without a step (fillet) and can be used to create ½-in.-thick loose tenon stock as well as molding profiles (see the drawings on the facing page).

To help prevent tearout, take light passes, gradually raising the bit until you're cutting at full depth. End grain is prone to blowout at the end where the wood fibers are unsupported. The solution is simple: Round over the end-grain edges first, then rout the long grain. Working this way removes any blowout that occurs on the end grain.

Hidden pull. You can use a cove bit to carve a drawer pull on the back lower edge of a drawer front.

⅜-inch-radius cove bit

Some router bits are designed simply to make decorative cuts. One example is the cove bit, which creates a simple concave edge. I use this bit often to create a hidden pull in a drawer front. Because the cove bit is designed

to make profile cuts, this choice is simply a matter of taste (I like the shape). You might choose a different profile, depending on the work you do. The bonus of having both a cove and a roundover bit in your kit is that you can use the bits in tandem to create a complex profile (see the photo and drawings on the facing page) or a drop-leaf table edge if both bits are the same radius.

Trim face frames flush to case. The bearing on a flush-trimming bit is the same diameter as the cutter, allowing you to bring a frame flush to a carcase using a handheld router.

½-inch flush-trimming bit

With a bearing-guided flush-trimming bit, ½ in. dia. is pretty standard, but you could choose a different diameter if you'd like. I recommend getting a 1½-in.-long bit, though, because the extra length comes in handy when working with thick stock.

The flush-trimming bit is indispensable for trimming face frames flush to carcases, and for trimming edgebanding flush.

With the flush-trimming bit, you also can duplicate pieces easily on a router table (called pattern, or template, routing). The bearing rides either against the original piece or against a pattern or template secured in a jig with hold-down clamps (see the drawing on the facing page). Before mounting the workpiece in the jig, cut away most of the waste on the bandsaw. Be careful not to rout uphill (against the grain), which could cause severe tearout. When you reach the point where the grain changes direction, reverse the workpiece in the jig.

Create identical parts on the router table. Cut away most of the waste on the bandsaw first, then place the workpiece in a jig with the template on top (see the drawing below). The bearing will ride against the template, making an exact copy of the original. Cut with the grain, and reverse the workpiece in the jig (if possible) when the grain changes direction.

Pattern-routing jig

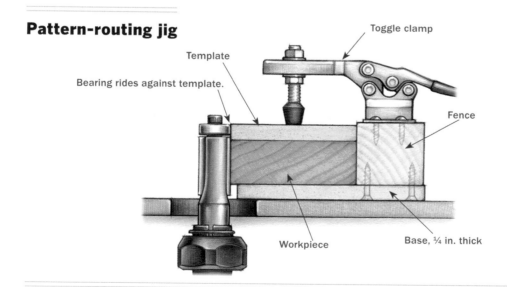

Template

Toggle clamp

Bearing rides against template.

Fence

Workpiece

Base, ¼ in. thick

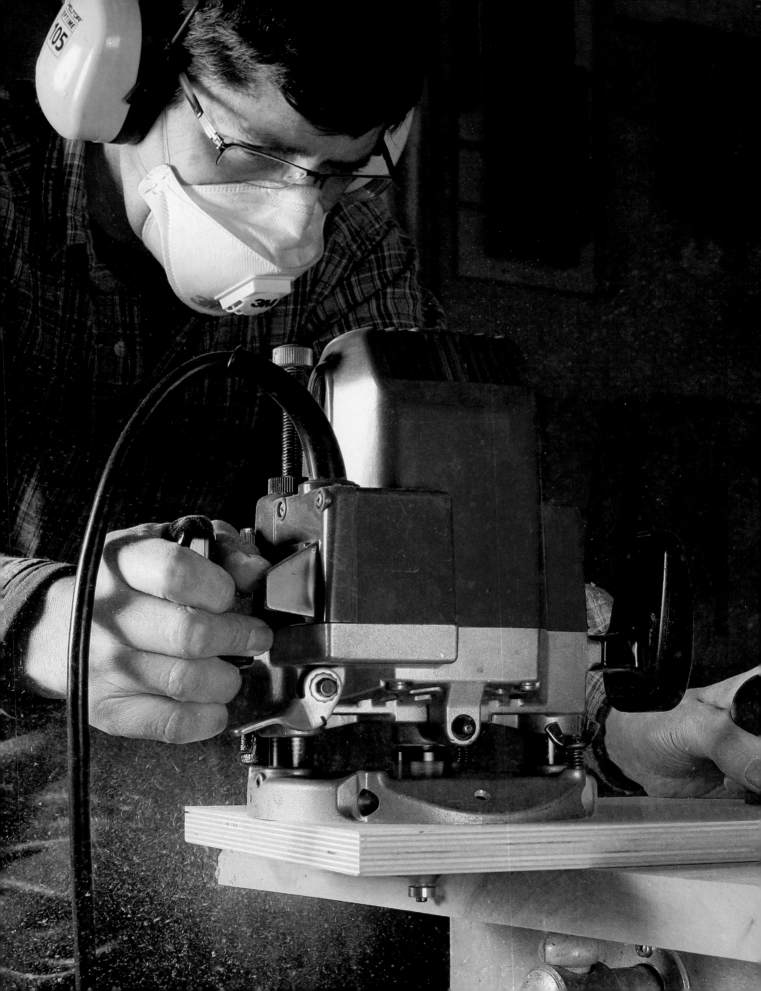

Upgrade Your Router with Shop-Built Bases

JEFF MILLER

A router is a very simple wood-working machine; at its most basic, it's a device that spins a cutting tool. This simplicity is a virtue, however, and is the reason the router is so incredibly versatile.

But the router needs some help to unleash its full power. One way is with custom bases. Once you realize you can attach your own sub-base to a router, you open up many possibilities.

The simple bases in this chapter help with a variety of tasks: They stabilize the router for otherwise risky cuts, they quickly and cleanly trim furniture components flush, and they make mortising a snap. The cost for this added versatility is a few scraps from your wood bin and the few minutes it takes to put each base together.

An oversize base for edge profiles

One common routing problem involves cutting edge profiles, an operation that puts more than half the router off the edge of your workpiece. This is manageable when the edge profile is small, but can be quite unstable with a larger router bit.

Wide base for edge-profiling

For better balance, a bigger footprint. An oversize base gives you greater control when routing an edge with large-profile bits. Use the router's plastic sub-base as a template for drilling the mounting holes.

Trim edgebanding

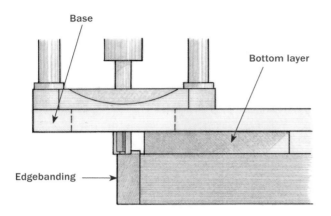

Base

Bottom layer

Edgebanding

Elevate the base. Adding a partial bottom layer prevents the base from bumping into the projections you want to trim flush, like the solid edging on the veneered panel on the facing page.

You gain a great deal of control over the operation with an oversize base, which helps prevent the router from tipping off the edge. This is important because even a small wobble can cause the bit to dig in and dent your perfect profile.

Start with a piece of plywood roughly 9 in. by 12 in. and drill or rout a 3½-in.-dia. hole about 2¼ in. from one end. Drill and countersink holes in the plywood so you can attach it to the router, with the collet centered over the base's opening. If you remove the router's existing plastic sub-base, you can use the holes in it as a template for drilling holes in the plywood. You'll need some longer screws that match the thread size on the ones that attach the existing sub-base; bring one with you to the hardware store to be sure you get the right size.

Once you've attached the plywood to the router, add a handle to the top side of the plywood, roughly 2 in. from the end opposite the router. I bolted on a knob from an old router, but a knob from a handplane or the like is perfect, too. Smooth and then wax the bottom of the jig, or use melamine board, or even a scrap of solid-surface

countertop material (such as Corian®), so the base will move easily on a surface. Rounding over the edges a bit helps, too.

Now you have a base that will give you the leverage to keep the router upright while cutting those edge profiles.

TIP A bottom layer with a straight front edge is great for flush-trimming dovetails.

Trim solid edging. The angled front on the bottom layer lets Miller work all the way into the corners on this veneered top. He starts with a climb cut on the outermost edge to reduce tearout. The bit is set to leave just a bit of edging to be scraped and sanded flush.

Smaller flush-trimming base. This square base is great for flush-trimming tenons and pegs. It offers support for the router on both sides of the bit.

Trim plugs and tenons

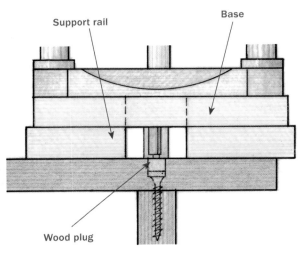

Two bases that simplify flush-trimming

The oversize base can be modified for trimming a row of projecting dovetails or through-tenons on the face of a board. Just add another layer to the bottom of the jig that extends all the way from the side where the handle is to about an inch shy of where the router bit will be. You'll have to press down securely on the handle, but this will give you access to rout off projections, where a standard router base would just bump up against them.

When you need to flush-trim in the middle of a workpiece, make a thicker sub-base that is square and just a little bigger than the base of your router. I made mine out of ¾-in. plywood, first attaching a square layer and then screwing blocks on either side of the bit to create a channel about ¾ in. wide (these dimensions will vary based on the specifics of the task). Set the router bit so it is just above the surface you're trimming down to.

Sure-footed. The base straddles a series of screw-hole plugs, for example, with the twin support rails preventing the bit from tipping into the work surface.

A self-centering mortising base

In use, rotate the router until each pin touches the workpiece for a perfectly centered cut. For mortises near the end of a workpiece, you might need to leave some extra length at first to support the pins.

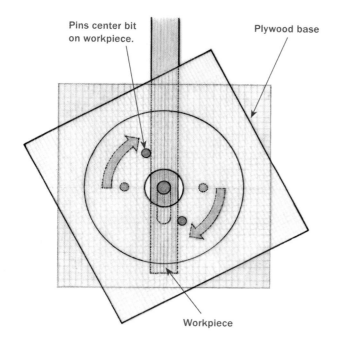

Pins center bit on workpiece.

Plywood base

Workpiece

Rotate the router. When the pins touch the sides of the workpiece, the router bit is centered.

This sub-base will support the router on both sides and prevent any tipping down onto the surface while you level wood plugs, for example. This base is also handy for pegs or other projections on a narrower surface like a table leg.

Centering base makes mortising quick

Another base, used with a plunge router, makes it easy to center a mortise on a leg or post. The base has two downward projecting pins at equal distances from the bit on opposite sides. The concept is elegantly simple: When you rotate the router so that the pins are touching the sides of the workpiece, the router bit is centered.

When building the base, it's crucial to locate the pins accurately. Do this after the base is attached to the router and a hole for the router bit has been plunged through. The distance between the pins should exceed the widest part you're likely to use it for. With the locations marked, remove the base and drill the holes on a drill press. Finally, insert smooth dowels—not the kind with ridges—or metal pins into the holes.

A better way to locate the holes is with a self-centering dowel jig, used in an unconventional way. With the base attached and the center hole plunged, chuck a ½-in. drill bit in your router (you won't be running the router with this; it's just a reference), then place the ½-in. bushing of the doweling jig

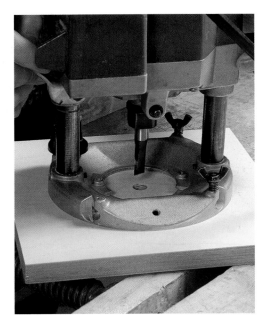

1. Simple method for accurate pins. First, plunge through a square base. Put a ½-in. plunge-cutting bit in the collet, and plunge down through the base.

over the bit. Align the ⅜-in. bushing hole so that it is either across or in line with the axis of the router handles, then position a straightedge against the jig and clamp the straightedge to the base. Drill through the ⅜-in. bushing into the base. Then swing the dowel jig around to the opposite side, use the straightedge to align it, and drill the other hole. You can then enlarge the hole for the router bit to whatever you need.

2. An unlikely layout tool. With a ½-in. drill bit chucked in the router, Miller uses a doweling jig to locate and drill the pin holes directly opposite one another and equidistant from the bit.

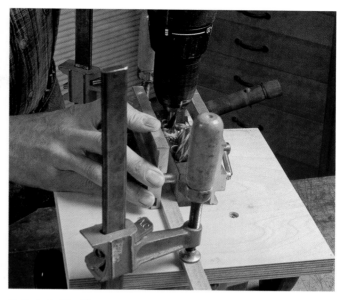

3. Register the jig on a straight strip. Clamp the strip in place and align the jig with it before marking and drilling the first hole.

4. Rotate the jig. After drilling the first hole, spin the jig 180° to locate the opposite hole.

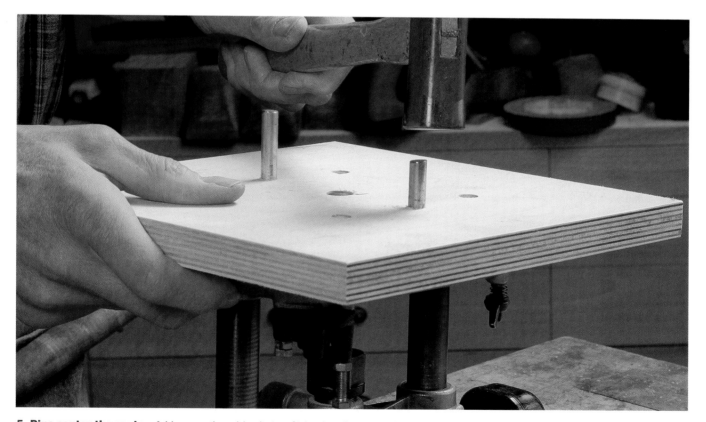

5. Pins center the router. Add some glue, drive in two ⅜-in. dowels or metal pins, and the jig is done.

Router-Table Basics

GARY ROGOWSKI

Contrary to what some woodworkers believe, a router is not the quickest way to ruin a piece of wood. In fact, when mounted underneath a flat table, a router is one of my shop's most versatile and reliable tools.

I began using router tables in the 1970s, shortly after seeing one for the first time and not long after I became a woodworker. The idea was an instant winner: a table or cabinet with a router mounted upside down underneath so that the bit stands straight up through a hole in the surface. The table's broad, flat top and square fence support the work and provide reference surfaces for accurate cutting. It's also easy to clamp blocks to the table for stopped cuts.

The tool's combination of easy use and accuracy has helped transform woodworking, especially for the small shop. With a properly set up table, a woodworker can produce hundreds of feet of molding in a single shop session. The user also can cut rabbets, dadoes, and other joinery, and—with the help of templates—can easily replicate shaped furniture parts.

Getting started

Time spent on setup will pay dividends in comfort and accuracy for years to come. To improve safety, minimize the opening around the bit and learn the right way to feed stock.

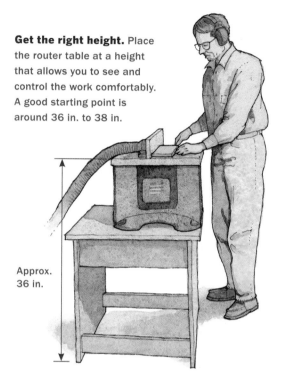

Get the right height. Place the router table at a height that allows you to see and control the work comfortably. A good starting point is around 36 in. to 38 in.

Approx. 36 in.

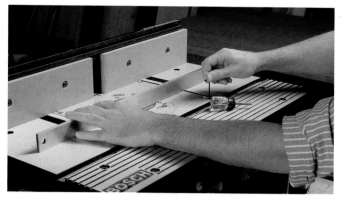

Make sure the insert holding the router is level with the surrounding table. Many store-bought tables are equipped with insert plates that hold the router in the table. Most can be shimmed or adjusted with setscrews.

Adjust the fence opening to fit the bit. A narrow gap around a partially exposed bit reduces tearout (left). For a fully exposed bit, close the fence completely so the stock doesn't dive into the gap (right).

Properly feed the workpiece into the bit. The work should move from right to left, so the bit's rotation pushes it into the fence.

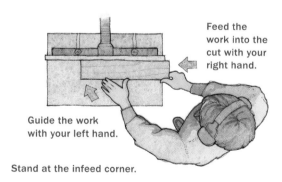

Feed the work into the cut with your right hand.

Guide the work with your left hand.

Stand at the infeed corner.

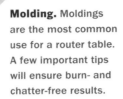

Molding. Moldings are the most common use for a router table. A few important tips will ensure burn- and chatter-free results.

Align the fence with the bearing. For a full-depth cut, the stock should ride the bearing without being pushed away from the fence. Adjust the bit height to make a series of passes.

Wide stock is better. When possible, cut molding profiles in wide stock to keep your hands safely away from the bit. A heavier workpiece is also less prone to chatter. It's easy then to rip the molding strip from the wider board.

There are a great many things that a router table can help you accomplish. Here are the techniques I turn to time and again for great-looking and accurate results.

Don't bypass the basics

When setting up and using a router table, you'll want to pay attention to a few basics.

Take care to set up the table at a comfortable height that lets you see and control the work. The older I get, the taller I like mine. On store-bought models, check that the mounting insert is flat and level with the table surface. Shim it with leveling screws or pieces of masking tape; if it's not level, you won't get a consistent depth of cut. The fence should be flat, straight, and square to the worksurface.

Always make sure that the fence opening is closed as tightly as possible without interfering with the bit. This will

ensure the best support for the stock as it passes the cutter.

When feeding stock past the bit, bear in mind a couple of things. First, keep the stock between you and the bit; in other words, don't trap it between the bit and the fence. Move the wood from right to left (into the bit's rotation). The rotating bit will try to pull the work into the fence or into the bearing on the bit, giving you good control and better accuracy. For most operations, you'll feed the work into the bit with your right hand and use your left to hold the piece snug against the fence or table as you move it past the bit.

For safety's sake, never put your hand over the bit area, even if there's wood covering the bit. Bits have been known to drill their way through a board. Also keep your hand away from the exit point on a through cut.

Use a push stick with smaller boards and use featherboards with thin stock.

In hardwoods, keep the depth of cut around ⅛ in. per pass. This avoids burning the stock and saves wear and tear on bits. You can make a deeper pass in softwoods. You'll need to experiment with feed rate, but remember the general trade-off: A slower pass yields a cleaner cut (especially in tricky grain), but a quick pass avoids burning the stock. End grain is especially susceptible to burning.

One bit, many profiles

A router table's moveable fence and bit give the user a lot of creative freedom. To see this flexibility shine, chuck up your favorite profiling bit and experiment a little. Interesting things are bound to happen.

The advantages are probably most obvious with a multiple-profile bit: Raise the bit and cut a bead on a narrow edge. Move the fence in or out to set the depth of the bead. Lower the bit and cut a double ogee in wide molding stock.

The same principle applies to simpler bits. Roundover, cove, or chamfering bits can cut edge treatments of varying depth and height, with or without small steps (called fillets).

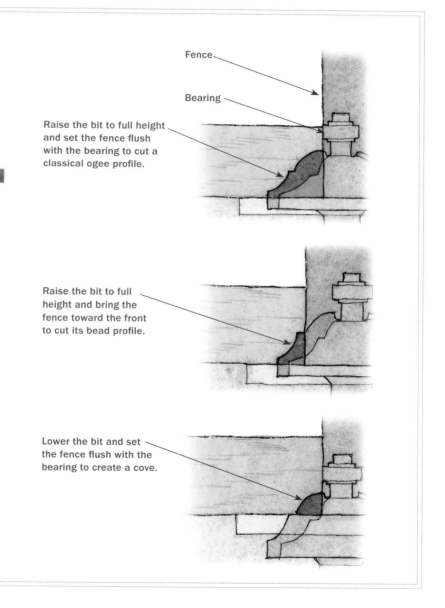

Fence

Bearing

Raise the bit to full height and set the fence flush with the bearing to cut a classical ogee profile.

Raise the bit to full height and bring the fence toward the front to cut its bead profile.

Lower the bit and set the fence flush with the bearing to create a cove.

Making molding is easy

The router table is great for cutting molding because of its large reference surfaces and because its fixed bit allows you to bring narrow stock to the cutter. Making such cuts with a handheld router is nearly impossible, either because the work is too small or the bit is too large for handheld operation.

When cutting molding in thin stock, use featherboards to hold the work to the table and fence. This keeps your hands clear of the cutter and makes for a more consistent cut—long, thin stock has a tendency to bow. An alternative is to mill up wider stock, cut the molding profile in the edge, and then rip it to size on the tablesaw.

Most edge-forming bits come fitted with a ball bearing on the shank that limits the depth of cut. For a full-depth cut, be sure to align the fence with the front of this bearing to avoid bumping the stock out as it runs up on the bearing.

It's also possible to cut several different profiles using a single bit by altering the bit height and/or setting the fence to expose varying portions of the bit.

Master straight cuts for basic joinery

A router table easily makes cuts parallel to an edge using straight bits, which means it is ideal for cutting joinery based on rabbets, dadoes, and grooves.

Rabbets

With the stock face down on the table, bit height determines the rabbet's depth and fence position controls the width, so a bearing-guided rabbeting bit is not necessary. Don't worry about the fence being parallel to any edge of the router table—the only

Rabbets. Rabbets are easy on all but the largest panels. For accuracy, be sure to keep the workpiece pressed against the table as it passes by the bit.

Cut rabbets in passes. Set the fence at the shoulder width and raise the bit incrementally.

important issue is the distance to the outside edge of the bit. If you're cutting rabbets deeper than ⅛ in., adjust the bit height to take one or more intermediate passes.

Similarly, when making end-grain rabbets to fashion tenons, set the fence distance to make the proper shoulder cut and adjust the bit height to gradually remove stock from each face. You can speed up the process by first bandsawing away the bulk of the waste.

Don't trim too heavily with the router. Remember that any adjustment in bit height will be effectively doubled if you're trimming both sides of the tenon to keep it centered. One way to avoid trimming too much at one time, especially when sneaking up on a snug fit, is to add a paper shim under the stock. If the fit is still too tight, then remove the shim and make another pass.

Tenons. To cut tenons on the router table, use the fence as a stop and the miter gauge to keep the stock square.

Tenons

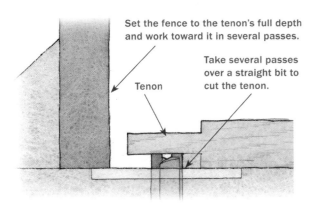

Set the fence to the tenon's full depth and work toward it in several passes.

Tenon

Take several passes over a straight bit to cut the tenon.

A tenon is a pair of end-grain rabbets. Any cross-grain cut will tear out as the bit exits the wood. Avoid this by using a sacrificial board on the miter gauge to support the fibers at the end of the cut.

Dadoes

You can use a router table to cut dadoes in short stock to support shelves or as part of a dado-rabbet joint for light carcase construction. Again, be sure to back up the cut to prevent tearout. The router table can't handle very wide or very long workpieces. As with rabbets, make multiple passes for deeper cuts. Be aware that most plywood is thinner than standard bit sizes, but special undersize bits are available. You also can use a smaller standard bit and make multiple passes (see the bottom photos below).

Router fence keeps dado cuts straight. For dadoes that are near the edge of a workpiece, use the fence to guide a clean and straight cut.

Dadoes. Like rabbets, dadoes are easy on the router table in all but the largest panels. Keep the workpiece pressed down to cut an accurate depth.

Remove the fence for interior dado cuts. A miter gauge with an attached fence keeps the cut straight.

Cut a dado wider than the bit. If you need a custom width or have a limited bit selection, you can get multiple widths simply by adjusting the fence between passes. But if you're making a lot of repetitive cuts, it's quicker to use a spacer between the fence and the workpiece. Make the first pass with the spacer in place and the second without it. The spacer's thickness should match the width you want to add to the cut.

Grooves

The router table can cut straight grooves in the edges of relatively thin stock, such as rails and stiles for a frame-and-panel door or tongue-and-groove joinery in slats for a cabinet back. With a straight bit, cut grooves with the stock held on edge. Or you can cut long grooves and tongues faster and more cleanly with a horizontal slot cutter, keeping the work flat on the router table and centering the grooves and then resetting the bit height to cut shoulders for the tongues.

Grooves. The router table offers excellent support for small workpieces such as door parts. Use push sticks to keep fingers out of harm's way.

Through grooves. Set the fence to position the bit in the middle of the stock. Then run the piece once in each direction. Any slight error will be mirrored, ensuring a perfectly centered groove.

Stopped grooves. Mark the outside edges of the bit on the fence. Measure from there and clamp the stop blocks in place. Lower the work onto the bit. When you reach the front stop, brace against it and raise the work. If your bit has no center cutter, move the work back and forth until you're down to depth.

Clamp blocks to the fence for stopped cuts

Stopped cuts are used in a variety of ways, such as housing drawer bottoms or hiding joinery for shelving or drawer dividers. A router table is ideal for cutting these joints because its fence is the perfect attachment point for stop blocks that define the limits of the cut.

First, mark your stock to indicate the end points of the stopped cut. Next, mark the diameter of the bit on the fence. The cut begins with the work braced against a stop that is clamped to the right-hand side of the fence. To locate this stop, set the workpiece so that the mark indicating the start of the cut is aligned with the mark on the fence at the left-hand side of the bit. Now clamp a stop block to the fence at the trailing end of the board. The procedure for locating the left-hand stop is essentially the reverse of this.

Start the stopped cut, pushing the workpiece tightly into the rear stop and gradually lowering it onto the bit. Then move it along the cut until you reach the other stop. Push against the forward stop and fence as you rotate the board up and out of the bit. Use a chisel to square the ends of the cut to the marked end lines.

Cut cross-grain first when raising a panel

To raise a panel on the router table, I use a straight rabbet cut; others make a traditional raised-panel bevel. In either case, make the cross-grain cuts first, then the long-grain cuts. This ensures that the long-grain cuts will remove cross-grain tearout. For thicker panels, make a series of passes to get to the final depth.

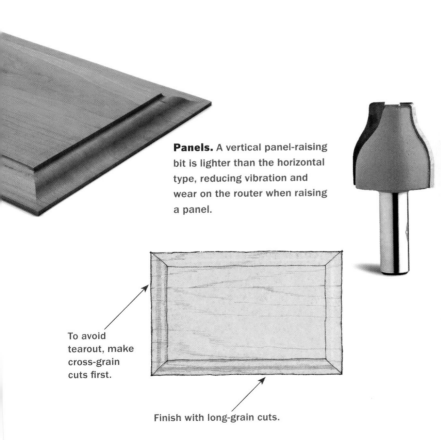

Panels. A vertical panel-raising bit is lighter than the horizontal type, reducing vibration and wear on the router when raising a panel.

To avoid tearout, make cross-grain cuts first.

Finish with long-grain cuts.

Use a tall auxiliary fence and raise the bit incrementally for a clean cut. Cut the end grain first, then the long grain. This removes any torn-out end grain at the corners.

Sliding dovetails

If the sliding dovetail is at or near a corner, such as on a drawer, the router table handles both parts perfectly.

QUICK DRAWER JOINT

A sliding dovetail joint is easily made
with a straight bit and a dovetail bit.

Start the socket with a straight bit to hog out the waste. Switch
to a dovetail bit and cut the socket in one pass (above right). Don't
change the bit height. Cut the tail with the bit set into the fence,
cutting each side in turn and sneaking up on the fit (right). Use a
backer board to eliminate tearout.

A CLOSE RELATIVE

The rabbeted dovetail is a half-version of
a sliding dovetail, reinforced with dowels.

**A well-dressed rabbet wears
dovetails.** Use a dovetail bit to
cut a pair of mating rabbets for an
elegant corner joint.

There are a number of specialized panel-raising bits for use in the router table. Some profiles come in large-diameter sizes only. Be careful using these bits—dial down the speed to keep vibration and wear and tear on your router to a minimum. Hold the workpiece flat to the table when passing it by the bit.

A better choice is a vertical raised-panel bit. These bits have a smaller diameter because the profile runs vertically. With this cut, you hold the workpiece upright against a tall auxiliary fence while the bit is captured inside the fence.

Start with a straight bit for sliding dovetails

Sliding dovetails are typically used for shelf support or drawer construction. For a ½-in.-wide sliding dovetail, first remove some waste from the female cut with a ¼-in. straight bit. Set up the fence so that the ¼-in. bit is centered exactly in the dado, and use a backer board if it is a through cut. Then mount the dovetail bit to the full depth of cut and make that pass. It will be centered where you need it. Keep the board flat as it goes over the bit. The matching cut is made with the board held vertically against the fence, without changing the bit height. Move the fence to capture most of the bit, and then adjust the fence to take light cuts until the boards just fit together by hand. The joint tends to jam, so tap the pieces apart carefully with a hammer.

A carcase joint—the rabbeted dovetail—is easily made with a dovetail bit. Use the bit to cut two mating end-grain rabbets to form a corner. The joint is an attractive way to attach a light-duty drawer front, but it has little mechanical strength. I add dowel pins.

To make the first cut, hold the board flat to the table and put a backer block behind it to prevent tearout. Again, the matching cut is made without adjusting the bit. The bit is captured in the fence so that only a portion peeks out. Holding the workpiece vertically against the fence, move it across the bit. Check the fit and adjust the fence accordingly.

Templates simplify shaping multiple parts

The ability to make curved and shaped parts is essential to fine woodworking, and the router table offers the fastest and most repeatable approach. You'll need an accurate template. Draw or trace your design on a sheet of thin stock such as ¼-in. plywood. Trim away the waste on the bandsaw, staying about ¹⁄₁₆ in. proud of the lines. Then trim carefully to the lines with a spokeshave, spindle and/or drum sander, or files, rasps, and sandpaper. Any imperfections in the template will be reproduced in the finished piece, so be sure to produce a smooth edge that matches the layout lines.

Before template routing, cut the workpiece close to its final shape on the bandsaw so that you're taking only a light pass with the bit. Templates should be fastened securely to the workpiece with brads, double-sided tape, or clamps. I use quick-action clamps to lock my work and template to a holder. I pass the entire assembly past a bearing-guided, flush-trimming bit to clean up the part. Set the bit height so that the bearing on the bit rides against the template. If the curve is symmetrical, there may be areas where you are cutting against the grain. This can cause major tearout. With my clamping system, I can rout the curve halfway, stop, flip it over, and then rout the other side of it, always cutting downhill or with the grain.

Template routing. A template makes it easy to duplicate curved pieces exactly. The bit's bearing follows the template as the cutter trims the workpiece to match.

Avoid tearout while template routing

Flip the workpiece end for end to avoid routing uphill and tearing out the grain on the wood.

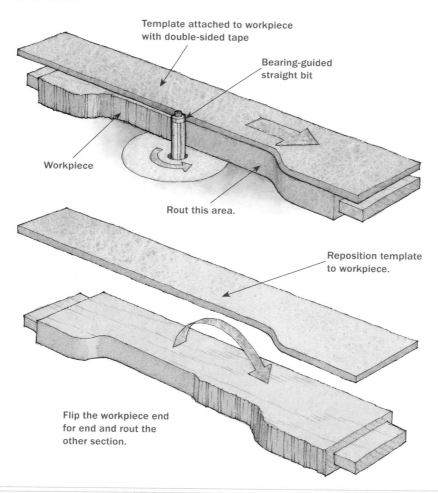

Template attached to workpiece with double-sided tape

Bearing-guided straight bit

Workpiece

Rout this area.

Reposition template to workpiece.

Flip the workpiece end for end and rout the other section.

A Versatile Router Table

KEVIN MCLAUGHLIN

Over the years I looked at a lot of router-table designs, but every one I came across lacked one feature or another. Shopmade router tables usually are limited to tabletop routing and fall short if you want to do anything more, like mount the router horizontally or use an overhead

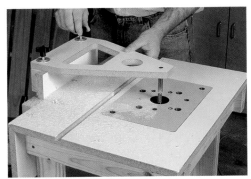

Adjustable carriage adds versatility. An adjustable carriage holds the router in its horizontal cutting position (above top) and acts as a base to mount overhead attachments, such as a pin routing guide (above bottom) for template-guided cuts.

Router-table construction

The tabletop and back are melamine and joined with a miter to provide a smooth, unobstructed surface for routing. The recess in the center of the table allows the router baseplate to sit flush with the tabletop. Size the opening in the top so that the router can be lowered in from above. The measurements in the drawing may need to be modified should you use different hardware.

Cutout for horizontal router bit, 4 in. wide by 3½ in. high

Cutout for sacrificial block, 3¾ in. wide by 5 in. long

Sacrificial block for horizontal routing

Melamine top, 24 in. wide by 18⅛ in. deep

Miter-gauge slot, ⅜ in. deep by ⅝ in. wide

Recess for router baseplate, ⅜ in. deep

Opening in stop block for sacrificial block, 2¾ in. wide by 3 in. long

Melamine back, ¾ in. thick by 24 in. wide by 8 in. long

Left and right upper rails, 17½ in. long

Ledge, 1 in. wide, supports baseplate.

Front and back upper rails, 17¾ in. long

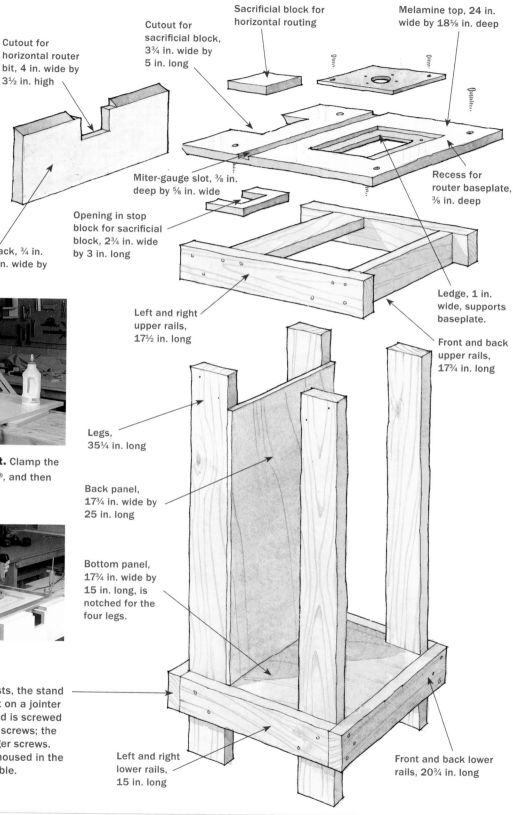

Legs, 35¼ in. long

Back panel, 17¾ in. wide by 25 in. long

Bottom panel, 17¾ in. wide by 15 in. long, is notched for the four legs.

Left and right lower rails, 15 in. long

Front and back lower rails, 20¾ in. long

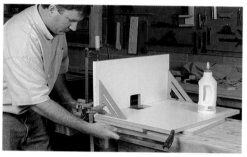

Framing squares ensure a 90° fit. Clamp the top and back to two Speed Squares®, and then clamp the mitered joint.

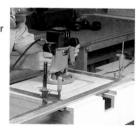

Rout the inset in the top. Clamp router guides in place, then rout a ledge into the top. The router baseplate should sit flush with the top.

No-Frills Stand. To keep down costs, the stand is constructed with 2×4s milled flat on a jointer and planer. The top part of the stand is screwed to the tabletop with 1⅝-in. drywall screws; the legs and bottom frame require longer screws. McLaughlin added a 25-lb. weight housed in the lower frame to anchor the router table.

The adjustable carriage

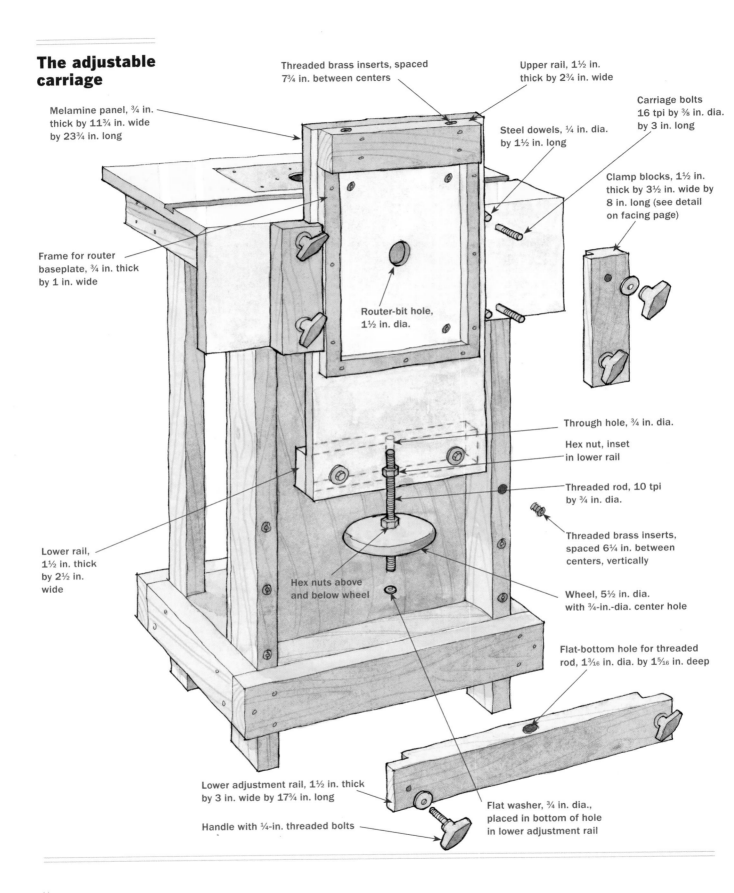

Melamine panel, ¾ in. thick by 11¾ in. wide by 23¾ in. long

Threaded brass inserts, spaced 7¾ in. between centers

Upper rail, 1½ in. thick by 2¾ in. wide

Carriage bolts 16 tpi by ⅜ in. dia. by 3 in. long

Steel dowels, ¼ in. dia. by 1½ in. long

Clamp blocks, 1½ in. thick by 3½ in. wide by 8 in. long (see detail on facing page)

Frame for router baseplate, ¾ in. thick by 1 in. wide

Router-bit hole, 1½ in. dia.

Through hole, ¾ in. dia.

Hex nut, inset in lower rail

Threaded rod, 10 tpi by ¾ in. dia.

Threaded brass inserts, spaced 6¼ in. between centers, vertically

Lower rail, 1½ in. thick by 2½ in. wide

Hex nuts above and below wheel

Wheel, 5½ in. dia. with ¾-in.-dia. center hole

Flat-bottom hole for threaded rod, 1³⁄₁₆ in. dia. by 1⁵⁄₁₆ in. deep

Lower adjustment rail, 1½ in. thick by 3 in. wide by 17¾ in. long

Handle with ¼-in. threaded bolts

Flat washer, ¾ in. dia., placed in bottom of hole in lower adjustment rail

Clamp-block detail

Carriage bolts and threaded knobs keep the clamps in place. The steel dowels keep the carriage in line.

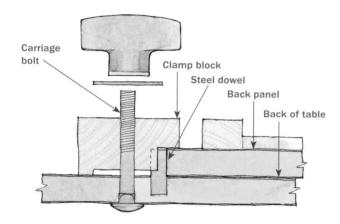

Carriage bolt

Clamp block

Steel dowel

Back panel

Back of table

A frame on the back of the adjustable carriage holds a router baseplate. The frame supports a horizontally mounted router. The upper rail also supports overhead attachments.

Mount the adjustable carriage to the table. Clamp the carriage in place so that it sits perpendicular to the tabletop. Drill holes for carriage bolts and steel dowels.

Clamp blocks secure the adjustable carriage. The clamp blocks fit over the carriage bolts and steel dowels and are tightened in place with threaded handles.

pin routing guide. The same is true for most store-bought tables.

My own router-table design combines all of the features I was after. The table I arrived at is easy to build, and it can be made with low-cost materials. Above all, because it accommodates the router in a variety of orientations, it can handle any cut that I could possibly think of making.

With the router mounted horizontally in an adjustable carriage, the table is set up ideally for cutting sliding dovetails or mortise-and-tenon joints. And shaping the edge of a wide board doesn't require balancing unwieldy material on end.

The adjustable carriage also doubles as a base to mount several overhead attachments. A pin routing guide makes the table useful for template-routing. A fence guard is easy to set up for safety. Finally, a horizontal carriage attachment allows the router to be mounted upright above the table surface and the work-piece. In this orientation, you can reference the flat side of the workpiece on the tabletop, which is helpful when

removing wide areas of material or when cutting irregular moldings. With such a simple system for mounting attachments, I can build new ones to tackle any tasks I think of down the road.

The adjustable carriage moves in a true vertical line perpendicular to the tabletop, so overhead attachments can rest on top and be moved up and down while remaining parallel to the tabletop, a design that's critical to using the overhead attachments effectively. This construction method differs from most horizontal router tables on which the router height is adjusted on a single pivot point, and the router moves up and down in an arc when it's raised and lowered.

The table is built with inexpensive materials

The construction of the router table is relatively simple. The stand is made of 2×4s held together with drywall screws. This is a sturdy and inexpensive method that can be modified easily if you want to add drawers or make an enclosed cabinet. Allow the 2×4s to acclimate in your shop so that they don't move significantly after the table has been constructed, and mill them on a jointer and planer to help the parts fit together squarely.

For the tabletop and adjustable carriage, I used shelving material from a local home center. The precut material is easier to handle, but a 4-ft. by 8-ft. sheet also will do. I chose melamine because it has a slick finish and is extremely flat. The various attachments are constructed with melamine and ¾-in.-thick birch plywood.

Start with a flat tabletop

Begin by choosing a router-table baseplate, and build the tabletop to accommodate it. I chose the Bench Dog® ProPlate. It has a simple design with openings that can accommodate several bit diameters.

Two ways to set the adjustable-carriage height. The position of the carriage can be finely adjusted with a wheel. Gross adjustments are made by moving the lower adjustment rail to different positions on the table legs.

Useful accessories

This router table can be modified easily to accommodate various routing tasks. With the router mounted upside down in the table, you can make use of several overhead attachments. For example, a pin guide allows for easy template-routing. McLaughlin built four attachments for his router table, shown here and on the next two pages. They follow only one standard requirement: They must attach to the top of the adjustable carriage with two threaded bolts with handles that are placed 7¾ in. apart from center to center.

OVERHEAD ROUTER CARRIAGE

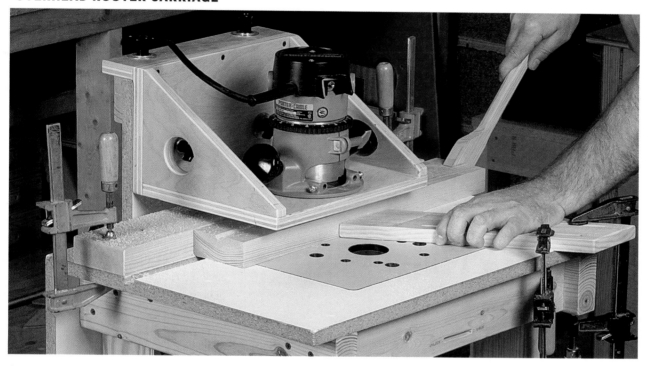

An overhead router carriage holds the router upright above the table, allowing the flat side of a workpiece to be referenced on the tabletop.

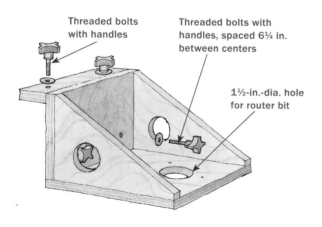

Threaded bolts with handles

Threaded bolts with handles, spaced 6¼ in. between centers

1½-in.-dia. hole for router bit

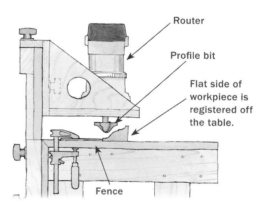

Router

Profile bit

Flat side of workpiece is registered off the table.

Fence

Useful accessories (continued)

PIN ROUTING GUIDE

A steel dowel, positioned in line with a non-bearing straight router bit, is used for template-routing. The template is guided along the pin, while the router bit cuts the workpiece to match. The pin guide is attached to the adjustable carriage. First, locate the hole for the pin by lowering the carriage while the router is running. When the bit hits the attachment, the dimple left behind pinpoints the location of the pin.

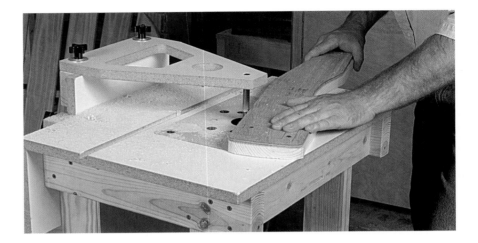

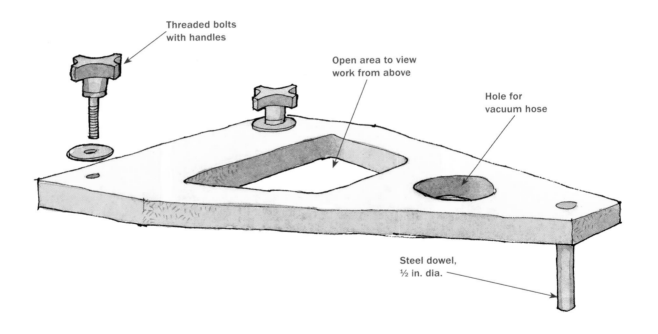

Threaded bolts with handles

Open area to view work from above

Hole for vacuum hose

Steel dowel, ½ in. dia.

The router-table top consists of a horizontal surface and a vertical back piece that are joined with a mitered edge. Care must be taken to ensure the top and back join at a perfect 90°.

Rough-cut the pieces ⅛ in. oversize, and trim them to exact dimensions using a router and a flush-trimming bit. This method will leave a clean edge on the melamine, unlike a tablesaw blade, which tends to chip the

FENCE GUARD

A clear plastic shield keeps fingers away from the bit when the router is mounted upside down in the table. A flattened 2×4 clamped to the table makes an adequate fence.

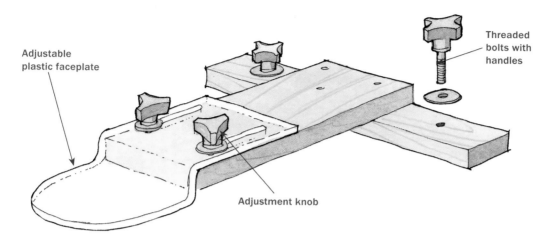

Adjustable plastic faceplate

Threaded bolts with handles

Adjustment knob

VACUUM-HOSE ATTACHMENT

This adjustable overhead attachment places a shop-vacuum hose right where you need it.

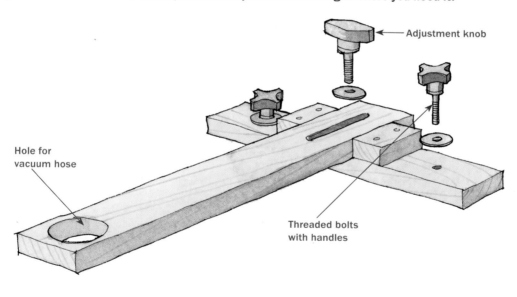

Adjustment knob

Hole for vacuum hose

Threaded bolts with handles

edges. Before assembling the two pieces, cut an opening in the back edge of the tabletop where the bit will be exposed when the router is mounted in its horizontal cutting position. This opening will hold a sacrificial block that can be replaced periodically. Once the opening has been cut, the top and back can be glued together.

Next, make a 2×4 frame to reinforce the tabletop. When building the frame, mill the 2×4s on the jointer and planer to get flat surfaces and right angles. This will prevent the top from warping when it is mounted on the frame. Assemble the pieces on a flat surface, and glue and screw them together. Then mount the tabletop to the frame with drywall screws and attach it to the stand.

Build the tabletop

With the top of the table assembled, make the remaining cuts on its worksurface to accommodate the baseplate and miter gauge. First, cut a recess into the tabletop for the baseplate. The baseplate must sit flush with the table, so the depth of cut is determined by the thickness of the baseplate. Cut the opening to match the baseplate. To do that, make a guide for the router to follow by clamping a straightedge and two right-angle squares onto the tabletop (see the top photo on p. 63).

Within the area that has been recessed, use a jigsaw to cut the opening for the router housing. I have a dedicated router that I use with this table, and I find it's easiest to just drop it into the table from above with the baseplate attached. This requires that the router opening be cut with enough clearance to accept the machine. You should leave at least a 1-in. ledge at the narrowest spot to support the baseplate.

Finally, cut a slot along the width of the table surface for the miter gauge. Then attach the top and frame to the stand.

Construct the adjustable carriage

Cut the melamine back panel to size, then attach a frame to its back side. The frame not only holds the router in a horizontal position, ensuring that the router does not shift during use, but it also strengthens the back panel. Install two threaded brass inserts inside the frame for mounting the baseplate. Finally, drill a hole with a Forstner bit through the back panel where the router bit will be exposed.

The carriage has an upper rail to support overhead attachments. A lower rail is attached to the bottom edge of the carriage to house one end of the system for finely adjusting the height of the carriage.

Set up the adjustable carriage to slide vertically

The carriage is held in place with four steel ¼-in.-dia. dowels and two L-shaped wood clamp blocks, which secure it to the table.

To make the sliding assembly, drill and drive the steel dowels into the back of the tabletop. The back panel of the carriage should be snug between the pins to prevent it from moving from side to side. The clamp blocks fit over the dowels and are further secured to the back with threaded bolts with handles. Loosening the bolts allows the carriage to slide up and down. Tightening the bolts secures the carriage in place.

Build the system for making fine height adjustments

Fine adjustments are made by turning a wooden wheel that's attached to a threaded rod. The lower rail on the adjustable carriage accepts one end of the threaded rod. Another rail is bolted to the legs to accept the other end of the threaded rod.

When constructing the adjustment system, use a ¾-in.-dia. 10-tpi threaded rod. One full turn of the wheel will move the carriage up or down $\frac{1}{10}$ in. For large adjustments, pairs of brass inserts in three positions along the legs allow the rail to be unbolted and repositioned manually. Set in the lowest position, the top edge of the carriage should sit flush with the tabletop. The other positions will raise the carriage enough to mount the overhead attachments. The brass inserts can be set in various positions to accommodate attachments of your own design.

Space-Saving Router Table

JOHN WHITE

I've seen many tablesaw extension wings turned into router tables, and it's not a bad idea on paper. You get an indispensable woodworking machine without consuming an extra inch of shop space. And you can take advantage of the solid, accurate fence already in place on the saw (or so you think). But it's not enough to simply drop a router plate into the melamine extension wing. For one thing, the rip fence is not ready for routing. Not only is it too short for vertical jobs like sliding dovetails, but the bit also must be buried in the fence for most tasks, and screwing a couple of

Versatile fence

Great dust collection

Up-top adjustability

Just screws and plywood

Use lightweight MDF for a flat, smooth top and plywood for everything else, assembling the pieces with drywall screws. A dust box beneath the table connects to one in the fence, so you can attach a shop vacuum below but collect dust from above, too. Replaceable inserts and faces will add years to the fence's service.

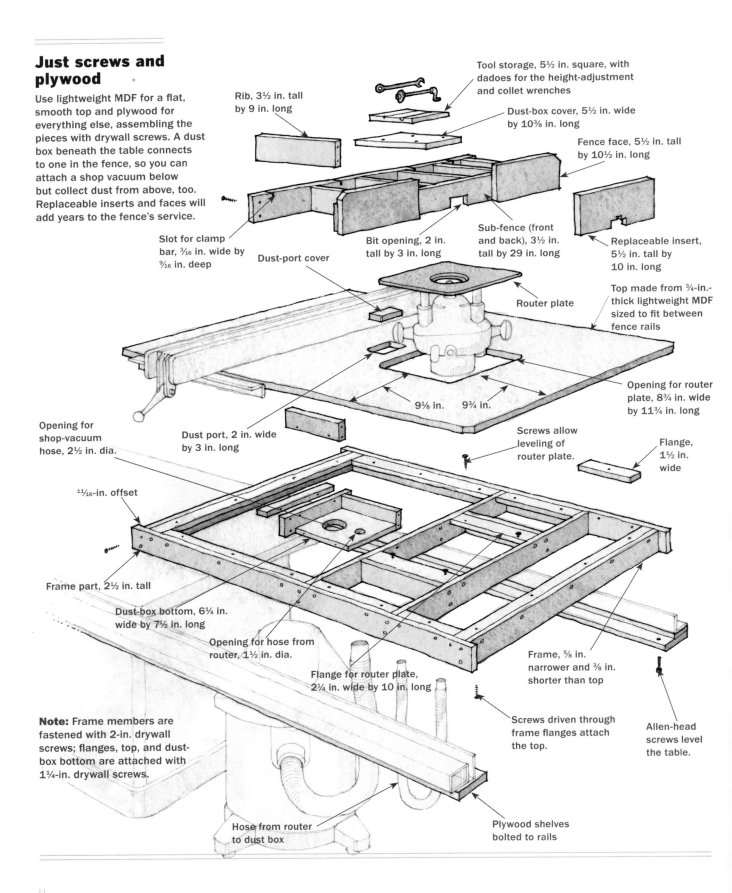

Tool storage, 5½ in. square, with dadoes for the height-adjustment and collet wrenches

Dust-box cover, 5½ in. wide by 10⅜ in. long

Fence face, 5½ in. tall by 10½ in. long

Rib, 3½ in. tall by 9 in. long

Sub-fence (front and back), 3½ in. tall by 29 in. long

Replaceable insert, 5½ in. tall by 10 in. long

Slot for clamp bar, ³⁄₁₆ in. wide by ⁹⁄₁₆ in. deep

Bit opening, 2 in. tall by 3 in. long

Dust-port cover

Router plate

Top made from ¾-in.-thick lightweight MDF sized to fit between fence rails

9⅛ in.   9¾ in.

Opening for router plate, 8¾ in. wide by 11¾ in. long

Opening for shop-vacuum hose, 2½ in. dia.

Dust port, 2 in. wide by 3 in. long

Screws allow leveling of router plate.

Flange, 1½ in. wide

¹¹⁄₁₆-in. offset

Frame part, 2½ in. tall

Dust-box bottom, 6¼ in. wide by 7½ in. long

Opening for hose from router, 1½ in. dia.

Flange for router plate, 2¼ in. wide by 10 in. long

Frame, ⅝ in. narrower and ⅜ in. shorter than top

Screws driven through frame flanges attach the top.

Allen-head screws level the table.

Note: Frame members are fastened with 2-in. drywall screws; flanges, top, and dust-box bottom are attached with 1¼-in. drywall screws.

Hose from router to dust box

Plywood shelves bolted to rails

Make an accurate opening for the router plate

Rout the opening flush to the template. Cut away most of the waste with a jigsaw, leaving about ¼ in. to be removed by a bottom-bearing, flush-trimming bit. Use a ¾-in.-dia. bit so that the corner radius matches the radius on the plate's corners.

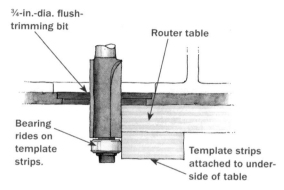

¾-in.-dia. flush-trimming bit

Router table

Bearing rides on template strips.

Template strips attached to underside of table

Build a routing template around the plate. Press the plate firmly against two sides, but use business cards between the plate and the other two sides. The extra space makes it easier to get the plate in and out.

TOP VIEW

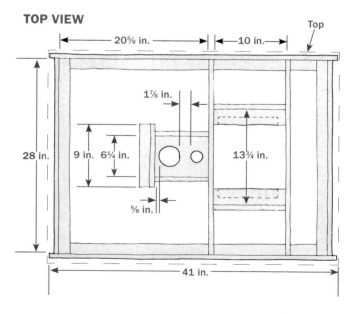

20⅝ in.

10 in.

Top

1⅞ in.

28 in.

9 in. 6¼ in.

13¾ in.

⅝ in.

41 in.

Add legs for support

If your extension table doesn't have legs already, you might need to add some. The table's cantilevered weight could be enough to make your saw prone to tipping over.

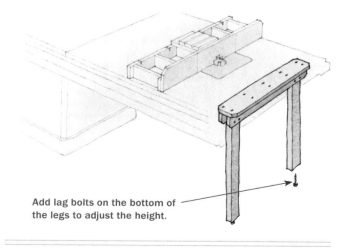

Add lag bolts on the bottom of the legs to adjust the height.

Have a smaller tablesaw extension?

If your saw has 30-in. rails, there won't be enough room to fit a dust-collection box behind the opening for the router plate. Instead, collect dust from the top of the fence.

Smaller Table

Shrink the area behind the plate so that the table fits the shorter rails.

Keep dimensions from the router plate forward the same as for the larger table.

Top

*For this version, don't rout the small dust-collection port in the table.

Modified Fence

Drill a hole in the dust-collection box cover for the shop-vacuum hose.

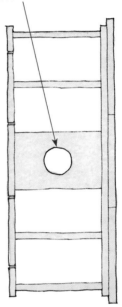

scraps to the back of the rip fence just doesn't cut it. Dust collection also is a problem, because there's no efficient way to collect from above the table. And single-layer tables eventually begin to sag under the weight of the router.

This router table solves all of those problems and a few more. First, it has a simple but effective fence that is tall enough for vertical routing. There is a replaceable insert, so you can bury bits in the fence and

get zero-clearance routing when you need it. The fence clamps to the tablesaw's rip fence, so adjustments are easy. Plus, it's a snap to put on and take off. Above-the-table dust collection is integrated into the fence—and it really works. Finally, a rigid plywood frame under the table eliminates sag.

The router matters, too

I chose a Triton router that specializes in table-routing. It allows above-the-table bit

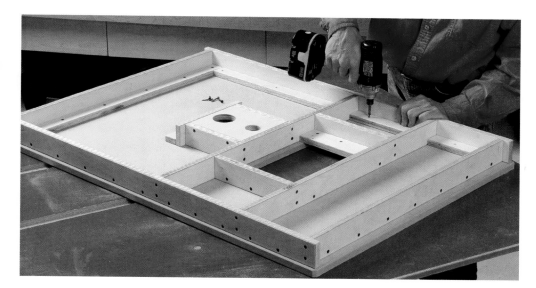

Solid assembly. The flanges serve double duty here. Not only do you screw through them, but they also provide a good bearing surface for the top, which helps to keep it flat.

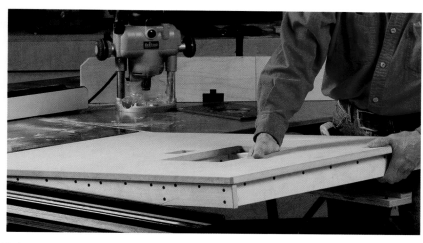

Plywood shelves support the table. Use nuts and bolts to attach the plywood shelves to the fence rails (above left). Lower the table into place (above right). It rests on the plywood shelves and gravity holds it in place.

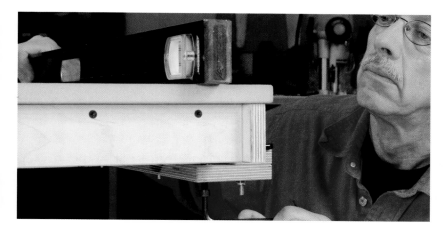

A screw in each corner fine-tunes the height. A long level lets you know when you've got it right. White filed a notch in the tip of an extra screw to cut threads in the plywood.

Same trick for the router plate. To level the router plate, White uses a drywall screw in each corner. The drywall screw will thread its own hole.

Ribs make the fence rigid. Clamp a plywood spacer next to the rib so that it remains vertical as you screw it in place.

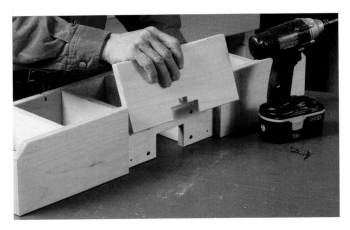

Insert is replaceable. Four screws hold it in place from behind. Make one for each of your most common bits to eliminate tearout. The tall fences on both sides can be replaced, too.

changes and height adjustments, which will save you hours of hassle. It also has dust collection of its own, so you can catch dust from beneath the table, too, making most jobs practically dust-free. To avoid the hassle of attaching the router directly to the table, I used a predrilled router plate from Rockler®. I used Baltic-birch plywood for the table's support frame and fence because it is stable and holds screws very well, and I used lightweight MDF for the top because it routs well and makes a smooth, durable work surface. One sheet of each is more than enough to make the entire table.

Make the table first

The table has two parts: a large top and its underlying frame with integrated dust collection and support for the router plate. Make the frame and then the top.

The frame is a simple affair. Strips of plywood—all ripped to the same width— are butt-joined and held together with 2-in.-long drywall screws. The joint is strong and no glue is needed. After assembling the basic frame, attach the flanges. Use 1¼-in. drywall screws, driven in from the outside of the frame, and predrill clearance holes and countersinks. Finally, assemble the frame for the dust-collection box. The box's bottom gets two holes: one for the hose that runs to your shop vacuum and one for the hose that runs from the router to the box. Running both hoses into this box means that a single shop vacuum can collect dust from above the table (through a port routed in the top) and below it without joining three different hoses to one another.

You'll need to rout two openings in the table, one for the router plate and one for the dust port, but neither is difficult. Begin by laying out their locations on the underside. For the dust port, simply attach template strips on your layout lines, rough-cut the opening, and rout it flush to the strips. The opening for the router plate must be more precise, but I have a great trick for that (see p. 73). After both openings are routed, attach the frame to the top.

Make the fence and install the table

The fence is assembled just like the frame, with butt joints and screws. Before you screw

Screw the router to the plate and just drop it in. Gravity will hold the plate in place.

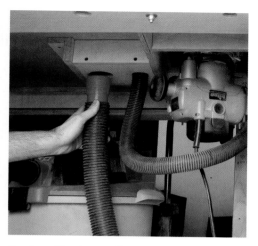

Hook up the dust collection. A shop vacuum is strong enough to collect dust from above the table and from the router at the same time, leaving very little behind.

Dust Collection

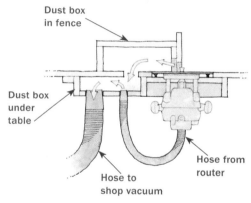

Dust box in fence

Dust box under table

Hose from router

Hose to shop vacuum

it together, cut a bit opening in the front sub-fence and slots for the clamp bars in the rear one. The fence faces are screwed to the sub-fence with 1¼-in. drywall screws, six per face. The replaceable insert fits between the two faces and is screwed in place. To create suction at the bit opening, attach a cover over the center bay created by the ribs, which sits over the dust port. Finally, cut two dadoes in a square of plywood—for storing the wrenches—and screw it to the cover.

To ease installation, I bolted plywood shelves to the underside of the fence rails. Next, I drove four Allen-head screws up through the shelves—one for each corner of the table—and set the table in place. I then laid a 6-ft. level across the saw's table and the router table and adjusted the screws until they were level. I leveled the router plate in a similar way, resting its corners on the heads of drywall screws driven into plywood flanges at either end of the opening in the table. After attaching the plate to your router and dropping it in place, attach the dust-collection hoses, clamp the fence to the saw's rip fence, and you're ready to do great work and do it faster.

Rock-Solid Router Table

PETER SCHLEBECKER

One of the first assignments I was given as the new facilities manager at the Center for Furniture Craftsmanship was to design and build the best router table I could using common woodworking materials. I started by coming up with a list of must-have features.

First, the table surface had to be big enough to accommodate large workpieces such as pattern templates for bending forms, angle-cutting sleds, frame-and-panel rails on the miter gauge, longer lengths of stock requiring featherboards, and inside curves. It had to be wide enough to resist tipping and shimmying when subjected to sideways forces. Also, the tabletop had to be extremely flat as a reference surface, and it could not

respond to the extreme changes in humidity that we get in Maine. It had to remain flat and could not deflect over the years or when heavy downward pressure was applied.

The top needed a durable, smooth, low-friction surface that would withstand the vagaries of student use. And I wanted the table-edge overhang large enough to support a clamp, without any deviations in thickness that would make it hard to get a clamp to hold properly. My list of basic considerations went on: The table had to be a good work height, and it had to be easy to change bits in the router and make fine adjustments. The fence needed to be flat and rigid, stay at 90° to the table, be easy to set and remove, have good dust collection, and be large enough to support large workpieces and the attachment

Panel raising

Template routing

Router joinery

The high fence fully supports tall workpieces as they pass the bit. The large surface accommodates small workpieces as well as tabletops, and the T-slide can be useful in creating joinery.

Start at the top

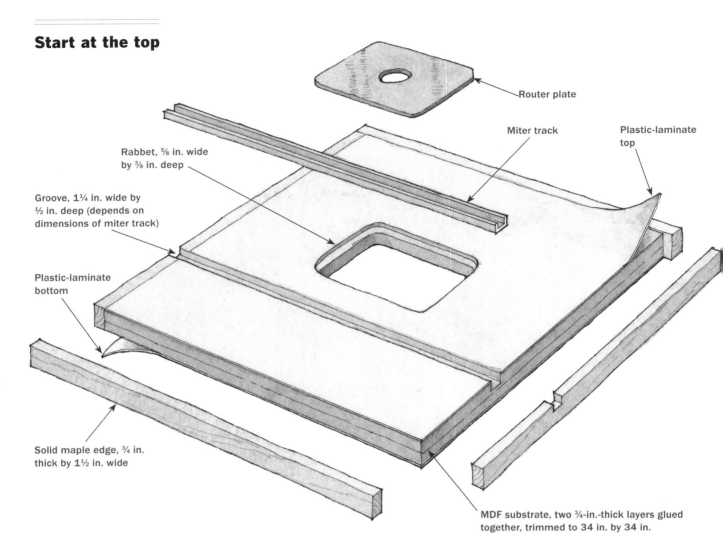

Router plate

Miter track

Plastic-laminate top

Rabbet, ⅝ in. wide by ⅜ in. deep

Groove, 1¼ in. wide by ½ in. deep (depends on dimensions of miter track)

Plastic-laminate bottom

Solid maple edge, ¾ in. thick by 1½ in. wide

MDF substrate, two ¾-in.-thick layers glued together, trimmed to 34 in. by 34 in.

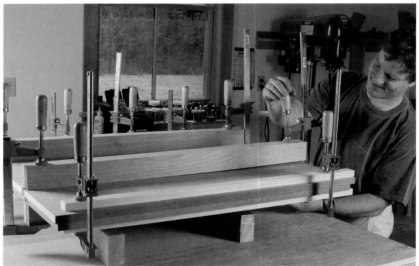

Glue two oversize MDF pieces together. Curved cauls help distribute pressure to the center while clamping at the ends. Trim this substrate square and to size afterward.

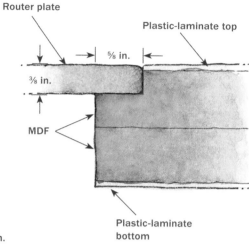

Router plate

Plastic-laminate top

⅝ in.

⅜ in.

MDF

Plastic-laminate bottom

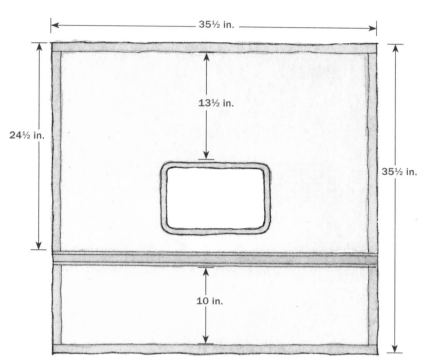

35½ in.

24½ in.

13½ in.

35½ in.

10 in.

Make an opening for the router. Drill starter holes in the corners and use a jigsaw to cut to a layout line. Make the opening 1¼ in. smaller than your router plate in both directions.

Sources of Supply

MITER TRACK
Bench Dog Tools
www.benchdog.com
800-786-8902

ROUTER PLATE
Woodpeckers®
www.woodpeck.com
800-752-0725

Woodcraft®
www.woodcraft.com
800-225-1153

1

of jigs and featherboards. The on/off switch had to be large and easily accessible for emergency shutoff, and the whole table had to be easy to clean, especially underneath.

We have had three of these router tables under nonstop use by students at the school for three years, and other than the routers being dropped occasionally, the tables have proved extremely durable.

Common materials, used wisely

The materials list for this router table is short: ¾-in. medium-density fiberboard, plastic laminate, plywood, maple, and poplar. For the tabletop substrate, I used a double layer of ¾-in. MDF because it is flat and strong. The MDF is sandwiched between two layers of horizontal-grade (thick) plastic laminate, which is extremely durable and seals the MDF from moisture. Using a light

Laminate the top. Apply the laminate top and trim all the edges. Dowels or narrow strips of wood (1) prevent the laminate from inadvertently sticking to the contact cement. Working from one end to the other, pull the strips out one at a time (2) while you smooth the laminate onto the MDF. Use a rubber roller (3) to apply even pressure across the top. The adhesive sets almost immediately, so make sure you have pressed the entire surface. Using a laminate trimmer (4), go around the outside edges, and use a starter hole to trim around the router opening.

color makes it possible to draw pencil lines for reference marks that are easily washed off.

The aprons and cross-braces make up a torsion box that supports the top and legs, and are made out of cabinet-grade birch plywood for strength, dimensional stability, and the ability to hold screws well. The legs are solid poplar for strength and nice edge appearance, and the design resists racking without stretchers.

I recommend a ⅜-in.-thick aluminum router plate that does not flex and has variable throat-size inserts to accommodate large and small bits. With an aluminum plate, you can be sure that the mounting screws won't pull through the mounting material. I use a router that can be adjusted through the base, thereby eliminating the need for a router-lift base. On the other hand, router-lift bases can accommodate a router you already have and are very accurate.

A simple top solidifies the table

Constructing the top is easy. You simply glue the two pieces of MDF together, add the laminate, create a rabbet to hold the router plate, and rout a groove for the miter track.

Recess the router plate. To make a template, surround the plate with four pieces of MDF and glue them together. Make sure the template is large enough to reach the edges of the tabletop for clamping.

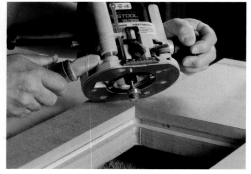

Cut a rabbet to hold the router plate. Choose the correct bit. With a ¾-in.-thick template, you'll need a short flush-trimming bit. Practice on some scrap first to set the bit depth to the exact depth of the plate. Then center the template on the opening and cut the rabbet.

First, cut the two layers of MDF about ¼ in. oversize so you can trim the whole thing once it is glued up. Use a few small nails in the MDF to prevent slippage (the nails can stay in as long as the heads are set), and clamp it in a vacuum press or with clamps and cauls. After the glue is set (yellow glue is fine) trim the top to size, maintaining squareness. Lay out the position of the router plate in the center of the top. Measure ⅝ in. inside this line to lay out the hole through the top. Now drill starter holes at the corners and use a jigsaw to cut along the inner line.

Next, cut two pieces of plastic laminate about ¼ in. oversize all around. Use two coats of contact adhesive on each surface to glue the top and bottom, letting the first coat dry until it is no longer tacky to the touch

Add a miter track.
Cut a groove for
the miter track. The
miter track should fit
snugly in the groove
and sit flush with
the tabletop. Various
tracks call for epoxy or
screws to keep them
in place.

but moving quickly once the second coat is applied. Trim all the edges, including the opening.

Router plate needs a perfect rabbet

Make a template from ¾-in. MDF to cut the rabbet for the router plate. Surround the actual plate with four pieces, making sure the final template is wide enough to clamp to the tabletop. Using a plunge router and a top-bearing flush-trimming bit with the same radius as the corners of the plate, cut the rabbet for the router plate. But first do test cuts, using the template over scrap MDF, until you get the plate just flush.

Edging the top with ¾-in.-thick solid maple seals the edges and provides a durable, softened edge. After applying the edging, the

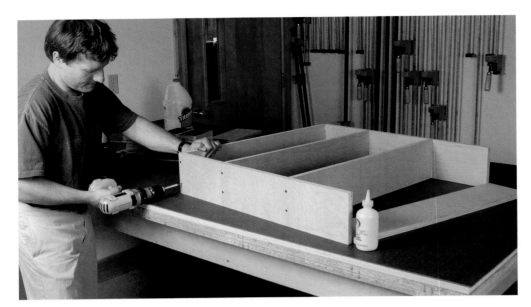

Glue and screw the sides and cross braces together. It's helpful to tack the pieces in place with brads first so they don't shift.

Add corner blocks. These provide strength and a solid place to attach the top with screws.

Attach the legs. Glue and clamp the legs in place before screwing them to the base from the inside.

final step is routing the groove for the miter track. This can be done with a fence clamped to the top and a router with a straight bit. The width and depth of the groove depend on the track you purchase.

The apron and legs are basic and strong

The plywood for the apron-and-cross-brace box should be cut very straight and square to create a level, flat torsion-box frame. I just glue and screw this together. It helps to use a pneumatic nailer to pin the pieces in place to prevent misalignment before the screws are piloted and sunk. Glue and screw in corner blocks for bracing and to provide a place to anchor the top with screws.

Mill up ¾-in. poplar for the legs. For visual appeal, I like to do a taper cut on the inside of the legs. We use this leg design on many of our worktables at the school, and it is very strong. Use biscuits to join the leg sections, and then glue and screw the legs to the apron from the inside to hide the screws.

When you attach the tabletop to the base, screwing through the corner blocks from below, make sure that the pilot holes

Assemble the base

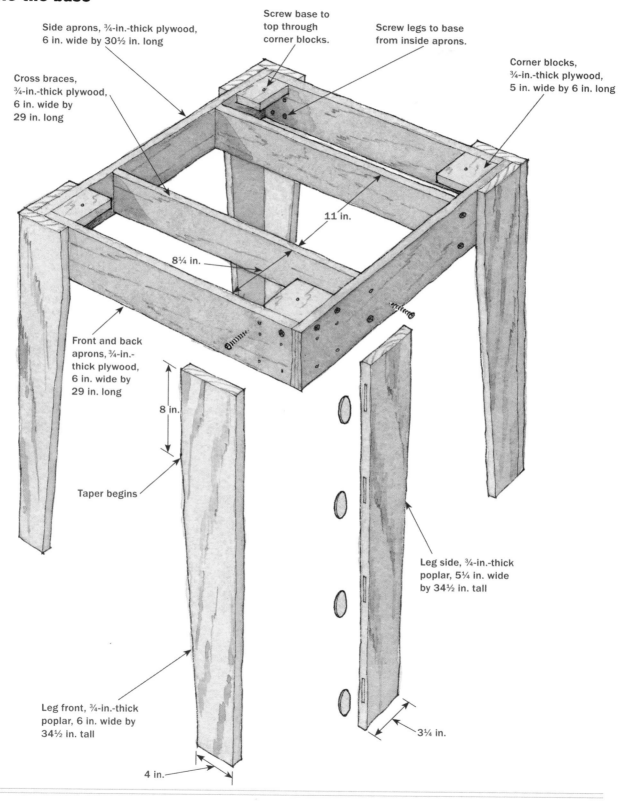

Side aprons, ¾-in.-thick plywood, 6 in. wide by 30½ in. long

Screw base to top through corner blocks.

Screw legs to base from inside aprons.

Corner blocks, ¾-in.-thick plywood, 5 in. wide by 6 in. long

Cross braces, ¾-in.-thick plywood, 6 in. wide by 29 in. long

11 in.

8¼ in.

Front and back aprons, ¾-in.-thick plywood, 6 in. wide by 29 in. long

8 in.

Taper begins

Leg side, ¾-in.-thick poplar, 5¼ in. wide by 34½ in. tall

Leg front, ¾-in.-thick poplar, 6 in. wide by 34½ in. tall

3¼ in.

4 in.

Make a sturdy fence

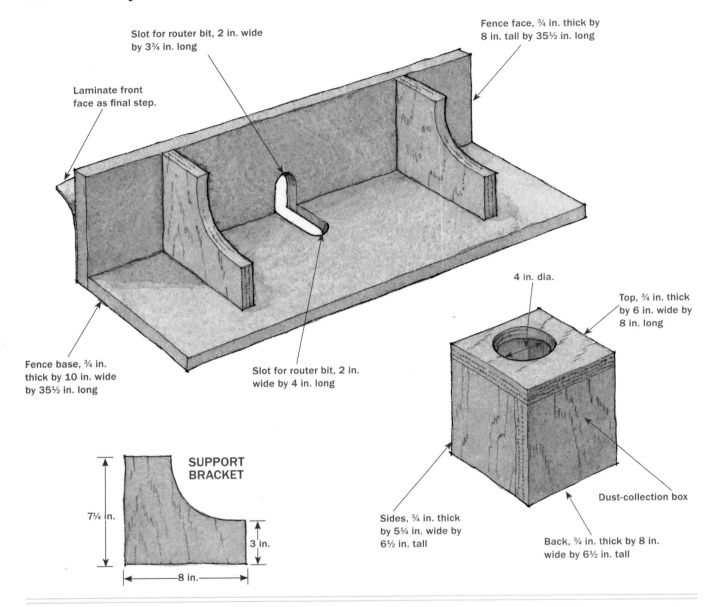

Slot for router bit, 2 in. wide by 3¾ in. long

Fence face, ¾ in. thick by 8 in. tall by 35½ in. long

Laminate front face as final step.

Fence base, ¾ in. thick by 10 in. wide by 35½ in. long

Slot for router bit, 2 in. wide by 4 in. long

SUPPORT BRACKET

7¼ in.

3 in.

8 in.

4 in. dia.

Top, ¾ in. thick by 6 in. wide by 8 in. long

Dust-collection box

Sides, ¾ in. thick by 5¼ in. wide by 6½ in. tall

Back, ¾ in. thick by 8 in. wide by 6½ in. tall

through the lower layer of plastic laminate are chamfered; otherwise, the laminate will crack. Now mount the router to the plate and install the external switch.

A high, square fence with good dust collection

A good fence is essential. It should be carefully constructed of MDF to be straight and square. I cut the bottom and face pieces out of ¾-in. MDF and the buttresses out of ¾-in.-thick plywood. Bandsaw openings for the largest bit you expect to use. You can always reduce the size of the opening with a zero-clearance auxiliary fence made of ¼-in.-thick material. The top of the dust-collection box should have a hole cut into it to accept the fitting for the dust hose.

Start with the bottom and face. Glue and screws are a fast, strong, and easy way to secure the face to the bottom. Squareness is vital to the fence's function, so check for square as you secure the buttresses.

Simple dust collection. Four pieces of ¾-in. plywood make up the dust-collection system. A hole in the top piece allows you to connect a dust hose.

Glue and screw the bottom and face together, and then attach the buttresses in the same way, making sure they force the bottom and face into a perfect 90° angle. Now add the pieces for the box using glue and a nail gun or screws. Be sure to drill pilot holes for screws to avoid splitting. The final step is to glue a piece of plastic laminate to the face using contact adhesive. The fence clamps to the table, so dedicate a couple of good clamps to it.

It's a good idea to add some useful jigs to go with the table: featherboards for narrow or long pieces, a corner dust chute for collecting dust when cutting an inside radius, an overhead pin guide for templates mounted to the top of a workpiece, and an angle sled for presenting the work at various angles.

Handheld Routing

GARY ROGOWSKI

Learning to use your first router is a little like getting acquainted with your first computer, cell phone, or iPod®. You've heard they can do so many things so well that you wonder if they can make a nice cup of cappuccino, too.

Well, not quite. However, a handheld router with a simple fixed base can cut edge profiles, joinery, and curves quickly and cleanly. In fact, it used to be that a fixed-base router was the easy choice for anyone making their first purchase.

The smarter move nowadays is the combination kit, which packages a single router motor with both a fixed base and a plunge base (for mortises and stopped cuts).

Bearing-guided bits for edge profiles

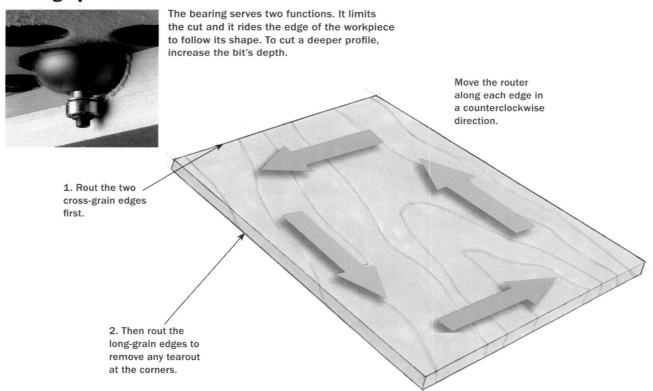

The bearing serves two functions. It limits the cut and it rides the edge of the workpiece to follow its shape. To cut a deeper profile, increase the bit's depth.

Move the router along each edge in a counterclockwise direction.

1. Rout the two cross-grain edges first.

2. Then rout the long-grain edges to remove any tearout at the corners.

For a few dollars more, this gives you plenty of room to grow and a great place to start learning. Even if you never take the plunge base out of the box (highly unlikely), the fixed base is versatile enough to take you a long way in woodworking. Let's see how far.

A few shopping tips

Routers come in different motor and collet sizes. Ignore the horsepower ratings and look for more amperage to get more power—12 amps should be plenty.

Most routers come with two interchangeable collets, ¼ in. and ½ in. Be sure to get a ½-in. collet so you can use bits with the beefier ½-in. shank. This gives you better strength in tough routing conditions and more bits from which to choose. Also, compare the ergonomics of the routers on your list before you buy. Feel how each fits your hands, where the on/off switch is, how well the locking handle works. These things will matter to you after you've spent hours making various types of cuts.

Cutting edge profiles

Bearing-guided bits cut molding profiles such as roundovers, coves, or ogees into edges using the bearing to limit the width of the cut. Some bits, like rabbeting bits, come with different-size bearings for making wider or narrower cuts.

Don't push the bearing all the way to the stock on the first pass. Make these profile cuts in a series of light passes to minimize tearout and reduce wear on the router. In fact, this advice applies to any of the cuts described here. Taking aggressively deep passes is hard on the router-bit edges. In addition, be sure to move at a decent feed rate

Add a fence for grooves. A fence attachment guarantees cuts parallel to an edge. A great way to modify this standard accessory is to add a straight piece of narrow stock for a longer, more stable fence.

Keep the fence tight against the workpiece. This ensures that the cut is straight, smooth, and parallel to the edge.

Make a jig for dadoes. Create a right-angle jig by attaching a piece of ½-in. stock at 90° to a 1-in.-thick crosspiece. Routing through the crosspiece marks the cut location, making it easier to align the jig with layout marks.

in long grain to avoid burning. Across end grain you want to move even faster, as end grain burns more readily.

Jigs keep the router on a straight path

Put a straight bit in a router, start a freehand cut in a board, and it will rout a sinuous course through the softest wood it can find. The router won't cut straight unless you make it cut straight. Fortunately, there are many ways to accomplish this. Most routers, for instance, can be fitted with a fence that attaches to the base and rides along the edge of a workpiece.

This attachment is great for making straight cuts parallel to a nearby edge, such as grooves to accommodate supports for adjustable shelving. Attach a longer auxiliary fence made of plywood or straight stock to give it better stability.

For cutting dadoes, a shopmade edge guide with a right-angle fence gives you a way of making the cuts straight and at a perfect 90° angle to the edge of a workpiece. This is especially helpful if you're building a bookcase or cabinet with fixed shelves. The jig is a simple straightedge with a right-angle fence attached. Plowing through the right-

Making the cut. The router's base rides the edge of the jig. To ensure a straight cut, avoid rotating the base.

angle crosspiece allows you to accurately align the fence with layout marks for each cut. Align the jig and clamp it to the work, with the fence snug against the edge of the workpiece.

One of the nicer tricks a handheld router can accomplish is jointing a straight, square edge on a board.

To do this, make a straightedge jig by screwing a straight piece of ½-in. plywood or

Make a guide for straight edges

Attach a piece of straight ½-in.-thick plywood or MDF to a piece of ¼-in. plywood. Use the router to trim the base parallel with the fence.

Trim base with router.

Fence

Base

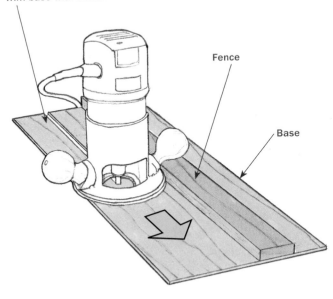

The guide keeps the router in line. Setup is easy, because the edge of the jig marks the edge of the cut.

MDF to a length of ¼-in. plywood. Use the router and a straight-cutting bit to trim the baseplate parallel with the jig's fence. This type of jig can be used to make any kind of straight cut, but it is especially useful for jointing an edge. Simply align the edge of the plywood platform along the edge you plan to joint, leaving a little rough stock showing along the board's entire length. Clamp the jig in place and rout the exposed surface with the same straight bit you used to make the jig.

When using this or any other straightedge jig, bear in mind that the router baseplate's outer rim might not be concentric with the bit. If not, then spinning the base during a cut will alter the distance between the bit and the fence, allowing the bit to go off line. To avoid this, take care to keep only one point on the base in contact with the fence as you move through the cut.

Cutting curves with a template

Pattern-routing or flush-trimming bits are straight bits with two or three flutes and a bearing mounted on them that is the same diameter as the bit. This allows the bit to

Use a template for curves

A bearing-guided straight bit rides the template's edge. The bit trims the workpiece flush with the edge of the template.

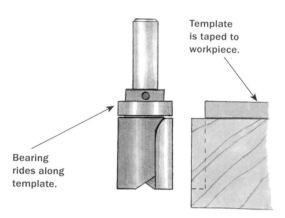

Template is taped to workpiece.

Bearing rides along template.

Thick stock requires a second pass

Remove the template and increase the bit depth. The bearing will now reference against the already trimmed surface of the workpiece.

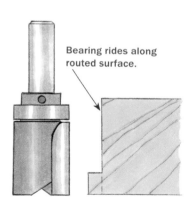

Bearing rides along routed surface.

trim a workpiece to exactly match the outline of an attached template, making it possible to cut multiple curved parts.

Carefully shape the template from hardboard or ¼-in. plywood, then trace the shape onto your workpiece. Cut out the shape on the bandsaw, staying about ¹⁄₁₆ in. from the lines. Next, use clamps, screws, or double-sided tape to hold the template to your workpiece. Move the router quickly through sharply curved areas to avoid burning the end grain.

Essential Jigs for the Router Table

PETER SCHLEBECKER

I've written about the router table I built for the Center for Furniture Craftsmanship (see p. 78), the school where I teach and manage the facilities. The primary goals of the design were sturdiness and a tabletop big enough to handle a wide array of workpieces and jigs. That was about making the table; this is about the accessories that go with it.

Easy to make and use, these five jigs and fixtures are some of the most useful router-table jigs at the school. With them, we repeat shapes consistently, quickly, and precisely. We make stopped cuts in angled workpieces, creating invisible and strong joinery. Profiling narrow stock is easier and safer. Edge-jointing a stack of veneers can be done effortlessly.

Safe and accurate. Featherboards are great for holding workpieces down, but they do not allow the workpiece to back up. If there is a problem in the middle of the cut, either stop the router or just keep pushing the piece through. Use a thin push stick near the bit.

Featherboard

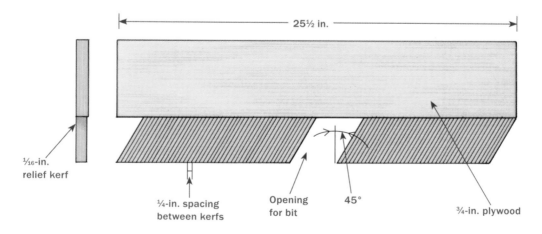

25½ in.

¹⁄₁₆-in. relief kerf

¼-in. spacing between kerfs

Opening for bit

45°

¾-in. plywood

1. Cut the featherboard in plywood. Reduce friction between the feathers and the fence. Before cutting the feathers, narrow the fence side of the plywood with a shallow cut, about ¹⁄₁₆ in. thick.

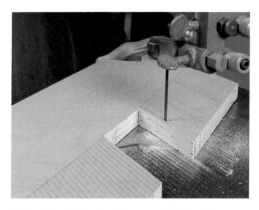

2. Freehand the feathers on the bandsaw. First, remove the cutout for the bit, and then cut the feather lines.

3. Put on the pressure. To have an effective hold-down that still allows the piece to move along smoothly, keep a little downward hand pressure on the featherboard while you clamp it in place.

Of course, if you don't have a router table like mine, you still can use these jigs. But if your table surface is small, you may have to scale down the jigs accordingly.

Featherboard: Manage small and narrow workpieces

Also called a finger board, this simple fixture holds a workpiece firmly against the table surface while a cut is made (see the photo on p. 97). It is particularly important to use if the workpiece is very narrow and there is a risk of getting your fingers too close to the blade. I use a featherboard for a pencil bead or for any other small molding, such as the slightly curved profile on dozens of pieces for a tambour door.

The configuration that works best for the router table is a long piece of ¾-in. plywood that is about the same length as the router-table fence, with feathers cut on both sides around a notch for the bit. Plywood is strong in every direction, so it allows you to orient the feathers along the side of this long board. Lay out pencil lines at 45° with ¼-in. spacing, and then cut the feathers on the bandsaw. The kerf will leave feathers about ³⁄₁₆ in. thick, small enough to flex well but still be strong.

To use the featherboard, put the workpiece on the table, apply light, downward pressure to the featherboard, and mount it to the fence with two clamps.

Pattern-routing jig: Fast, precise, and easy multiples

The most common use of the router table in our shop is pattern-cutting. Used for curved legs, aprons, or multiples of any kind, pattern-cutting is when a part is cut out using a bearing-guided, flush-trimming bit. The piece is roughed out slightly oversize on the bandsaw and mounted to the pattern. The bit then follows the pattern, producing the same profile every time.

Pattern-routing jig

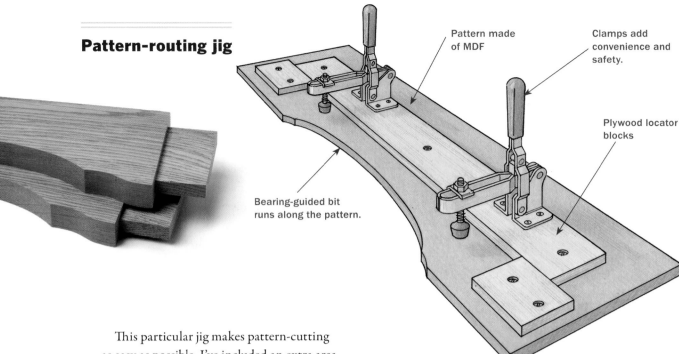

Pattern made of MDF

Clamps add convenience and safety.

Plywood locator blocks

Bearing-guided bit runs along the pattern.

This particular jig makes pattern-cutting as easy as possible. I've included an extra area before and after the pattern so the bearing has a place to ride as it moves into and out of the cut. I made it easy to locate workpieces instantly, and the toggle clamps hold the work in place and serve as built-in handles.

To make a pattern jig, draw the outline of the shape onto tracing paper, and then use spray adhesive to glue the paper to a piece of MDF. Use a piece larger than the shape so there will be room for toggle clamps, locator blocks, and start-and-stop areas for the bearing. Bandsaw close to the line and clean it up with power- and hand-sanding.

Position a blank on the pattern and surround the blank with blocks to locate it. Then use the jig to trace the shape on the blank. Remove the blank and bandsaw the shape, leaving it about ⅛ in. oversize, and return the workpiece to the jig. I usually install toggle clamps to hold the blank firmly.

When routing, begin the contact with the bearing on the pattern portion ahead of the actual blank. Follow through the cut to the other end; it's always good to take a second pass to clean up any inconsistencies left by sawdust and vibration.

1. Create the profile. To make the pattern jig, draw the shape on tracing paper and glue it to MDF. Bandsaw close to the line, and then fair the curve to the line with a spindle sander or a block and sandpaper.

2. Add the screw blocks. Position the blank and draw the shape. With the blank correctly located on the jig, screw locator blocks behind and on each end of the blank. Consider adding toggle clamps for extra control.

(continued on p. 100)

3. Rout the workpiece with a pattern bit.

Transfer the pattern to the blank (above). Bandsaw away the bulk of the waste, reinstall the blank in the jig, and rout (right). The bearing-guided bit rides along the pattern.

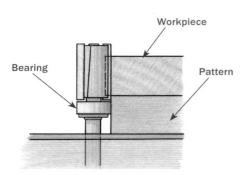

Bearing · Workpiece · Pattern

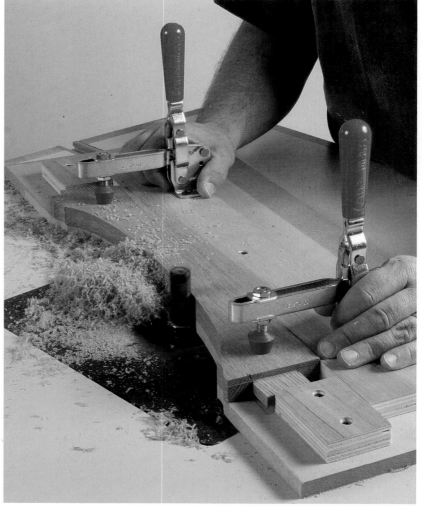

Pay attention to grain direction. A sharp bit can cleanly cut mild reversals in grain, but when the grain is steep and tears out, a symmetrical piece can be flipped in the jig to work the grain in different directions. If the piece is asymmetrical, make a second, opposite jig and flip the workpiece.

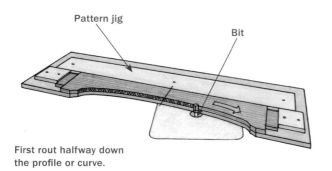

Pattern jig · Bit

First rout halfway down the profile or curve.

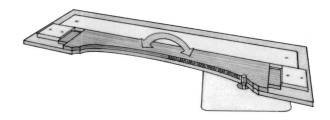

Then flip the workpiece and rout the other half.

Zero-clearance fence: For small workpieces

Sometimes workpieces are so short there is a risk that they will dip into the opening in the fence and cut too deeply, or that the leading edge of the wood will catch the outfeed side of the opening. A zero-clearance fence will prevent these problems and make the operation safer. I use this auxiliary fence anytime I rout a profile around a small drawer front or door. A bearing on the router bit could get in the way of the fence, so if there is a bearing, you'll need to remove it.

The zero-clearance fence clamps onto the regular fence. Make it out of ¼-in. Masonite®, about the same size as the regular fence. I use Masonite because it is stiff enough to stay straight near the center when clamped on the ends. After bringing the main fence forward of the bit and clamping on the Masonite, clamp one end of the main fence to the table. With the bit set at the correct height, start the router and then pivot the entire fence

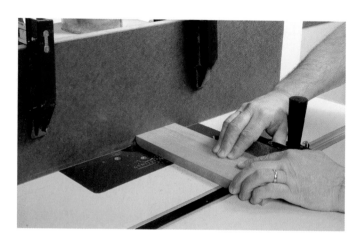

No room for error. A zero-clearance fence closes the gap around the bit and prevents short work, like this drawer front, from dipping into the open space.

Zero-Clearance Fence

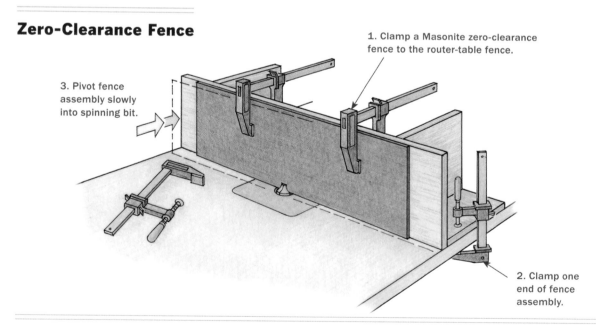

1. Clamp a Masonite zero-clearance fence to the router-table fence.

3. Pivot fence assembly slowly into spinning bit.

2. Clamp one end of fence assembly.

Miter angle sled

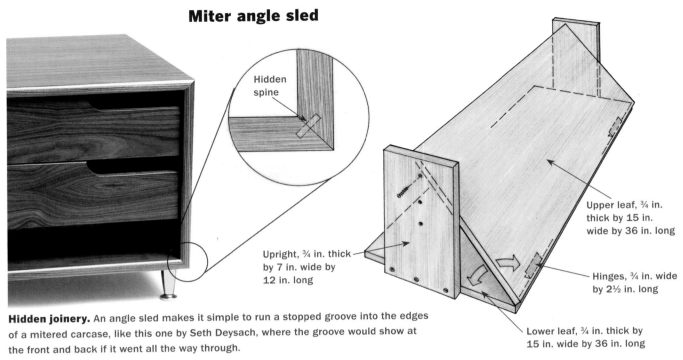

Hidden spine

Upright, ¾ in. thick by 7 in. wide by 12 in. long

Upper leaf, ¾ in. thick by 15 in. wide by 36 in. long

Hinges, ¾ in. wide by 2½ in. long

Lower leaf, ¾ in. thick by 15 in. wide by 36 in. long

Hidden joinery. An angle sled makes it simple to run a stopped groove into the edges of a mitered carcase, like this one by Seth Deysach, where the groove would show at the front and back if it went all the way through.

Set up the angle. Once the leaves are hinged and the uprights are screwed to the lower leaf, use a bevel gauge to set the angle (right), and screw through each upright to lock the upper leaves (far right).

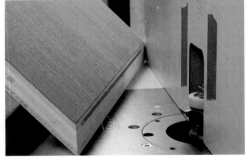

Use the fence as a pivot point for a stopped cut. With the workpiece clamped on the angle sled and the stopping points taped on the fence, use the fence to pivot into the bit on one end and out on the other.

Veneer jig

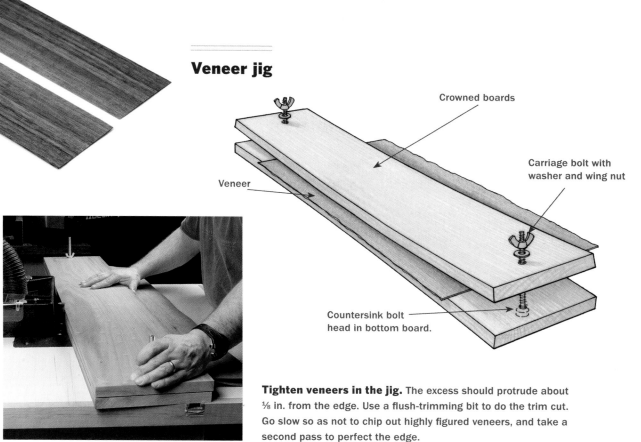

Crowned boards

Veneer

Carriage bolt with washer and wing nut

Countersink bolt head in bottom board.

Tighten veneers in the jig. The excess should protrude about ⅛ in. from the edge. Use a flush-trimming bit to do the trim cut. Go slow so as not to chip out highly figured veneers, and take a second pass to perfect the edge.

so that the bit slowly cuts through the hardboard from the rear. I bring the cutter just a bit farther out than needed and then back it off to leave a little clearance for the blades. This reduces heat buildup and noise. Stop the router, lock down the free end of the fence, and try a test cut.

Miter angle sled: Simple sled presents work at an angle

When it is necessary to present a piece of wood at an angle to the router bit, as with a mitered joint with spline grooves in box or carcase construction, this sled makes it easy. Cutting the grooves on the tablesaw is not an option if you want to make stopped grooves, hiding the splines. But this sled, used on the router table with a slot-cutting bit, will do the job perfectly.

Constructing the sled is simple. I make my sled big enough to hold a range of sizes with

extra space to screw in hold-down blocks should I need them. Two squared boards of sheet material are held together with inexpensive utility hinges, and end pieces establish the angle. The workpiece is clamped onto the upper leaf so that the leading edge just touches the table surface. Or you can align the side or top edge with marks or stop blocks screwed to the upper leaf. When routing the end of a narrower piece, the upright end can serve as a right-angle guide as long as the components of the jig have been made accurately square.

A router bit can be used with a bearing that will run along the workpiece, as in the case of the slot-cutting bit.

Veneer jig: Joint perfect edges on a stack of veneers

Edge-jointing veneers with a handplane can be time-consuming and frustrating. Instead, you can use a veneer-trimming jig to joint multiple leaves of veneer at the same time. I like this jig because it is simple, can handle any width of veneer, and is easy to re-true on a jointer. It consists of two poplar boards bolted together at the ends. For short lengths, two flat boards will suffice. However, for veneers up to about 5 ft. in length, I make a longer jig with a camber in the boards so that clamping pressure is even along the entire length.

To create the camber, square up two 5/4 boards to about 1⅛ in. thick. Set the jointer to take a ¹⁄₁₆-in. cut and run the first board over the cutterhead about one-third of the way along the board. Stop the motor, turn the board around, and repeat on the other end, same face down. Repeat this three times on both ends, stopping each time about 4 in. from the end of the previous cut. The board should be tapered on both ends in a series of steps.

Next, flip the board and use a planer to remove the material in the center until the whole board has been planed end to end. A planer won't remove the camber from the board, and the steps will not show up on the planed side. Flip the board and take a pass or two to clean up the stepped side. Repeat the process on the other board.

Drill holes for carriage bolts, making sure to countersink the heads and install washers and wing nuts. When the crowns of the boards are pressed against each other, they will force the whole jig to lie flat on the table surface. Lock the assembly down and run both edges over the jointer to true them up, and you're ready to insert veneer leaves and edge-joint them.

Crowned boards are the key.
Start with steps. Schlebecker takes multiple jointer passes on both ends of the boards, shorter each time. He tapes a mark on the jointer and matches it to lines on the top of the board to know when to pick up the board.

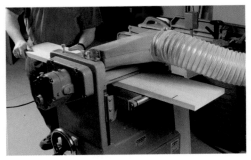

Plane it smooth. Next, with the steps facing down on the bed, he runs the board through the planer until the board has been planed across its length. Then he flips the board over and gradually removes the steps.

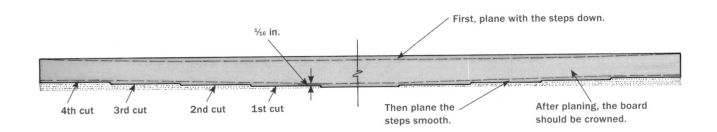

¹⁄₁₆ in.

First, plane with the steps down.

4th cut   3rd cut   2nd cut   1st cut

Then plane the steps smooth.

After planing, the board should be crowned.

Five Smart Router Jigs

YEUNG CHAN

Few woodworkers enjoy the luxury of a spacious shop, and I'm no exception. Lacking the space for many large machines, I rely on my router when building furniture. However, used on its own, the router is limited in its abilities. More often than not, I use it in conjunction with various shopmade jigs that increase its ability to quickly and accurately cut circles, make edge profiles, cut dadoes, trim edge-banding, and even substitute for a lathe.

The five jigs illustrated here are all made from cheap and stable plywood or medium-density fiberboard and require only a few pieces of hardware, available through Lee Valley® (www.leevalley.com; 800-871-8158) or Rockler (www.rockler.com; 800-279-4441). These router jigs are as easy to use as they are to make.

Set the size of the circle. With the pin registered in the center of the workpiece, move the jig's base until the inside edge of the router bit is aligned with the desired outside edge of the circle.

Cut perfect circles

The adjustable circle-cutting jig can be used to rout a circle with a maximum diameter of 72 in., but the design can be modified for other diameters. First, drill a ¼-in.-dia. hole, ¼ in. deep, in the middle of the workpiece. If you don't want the hole to show, work on the underside. Next, mark a point on the desired edge of the circle, place the sled over the base, and fit the jig's pin in the center hole. Move the base in or out until the bit is on the mark, then lock the sled.

Turn on the router and plunge down to start the initial cut, which should be less than ⅛ in. deep, just enough to define the circle. Use a jigsaw to cut away the outside pieces, leaving about ⅛ in. outside the final size of the circle. This method enables you to support the corners as they are cut off so that they won't damage the finished workpiece. Once the bulk of the waste has been removed, the router has to make only a light final cut. If you're working with solid wood, pay attention to the grain's orientation and the bit's rotation. Climb-cut when necessary to avoid tearout.

Adjustable circle-cutting jig

All pieces of the jig are made of ½-in.-thick plywood.

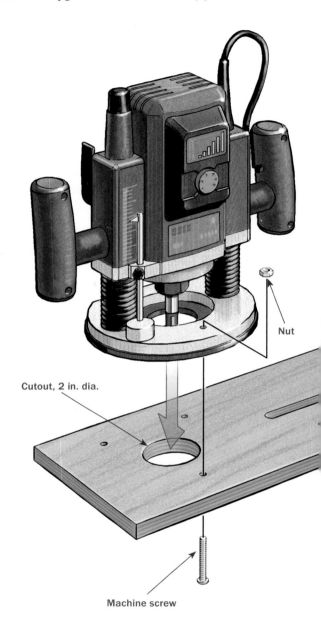

Nut

Cutout, 2 in. dia.

Machine screw

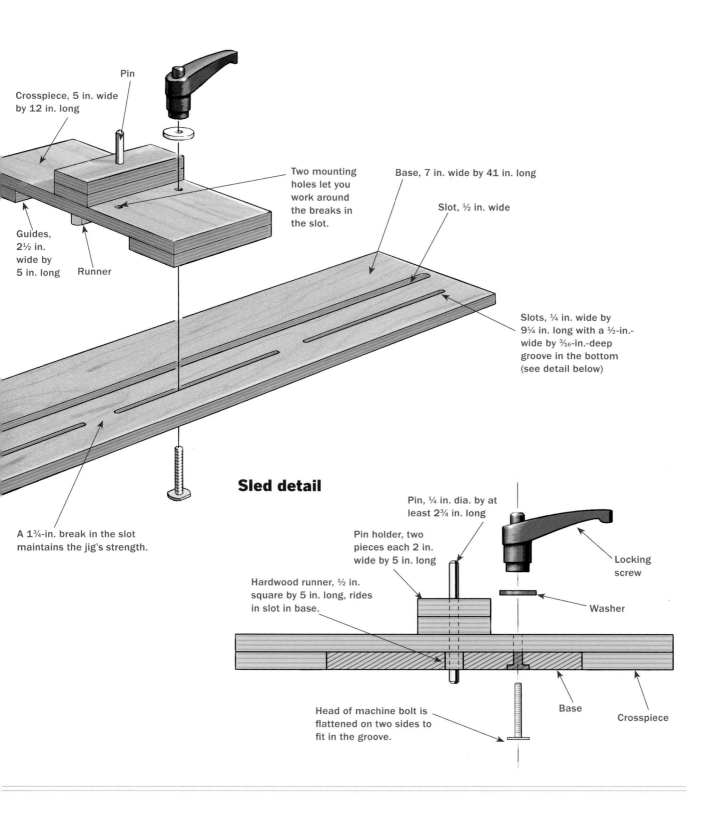

Pin

Crosspiece, 5 in. wide
by 12 in. long

Two mounting
holes let you
work around
the breaks in
the slot.

Guides,
2½ in.
wide by
5 in. long

Runner

Base, 7 in. wide by 41 in. long

Slot, ½ in. wide

Slots, ¼ in. wide by
9¼ in. long with a ½-in.-
wide by ³⁄₁₆-in.-deep
groove in the bottom
(see detail below)

A 1¾-in. break in the slot
maintains the jig's strength.

Sled detail

Pin, ¼ in. dia. by at
least 2¾ in. long

Pin holder, two
pieces each 2 in.
wide by 5 in. long

Hardwood runner, ½ in.
square by 5 in. long, rides
in slot in base.

Locking
screw

Washer

Base

Crosspiece

Head of machine bolt is
flattened on two sides to
fit in the groove.

Make a shallow cut to define the circle. The initial cut made with the router should be only about ⅛ in. deep.

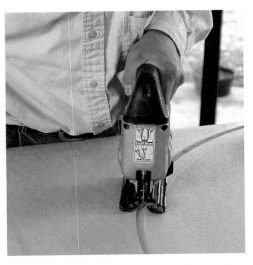

Remove the waste. Following the track left by the router, saw away the waste.

The final cut. The router now has to remove only a small amount of material, creating less dust and leaving a clean cut.

Trim or cut large panels

It is a difficult job to cut a large panel on a tablesaw that's not equipped with a sliding table. So I made a simple jig, the straight-edge jig, that can be used to cut out a section from a full sheet of plywood or medium-density fiberboard or to clean up a rough cut made by a jigsaw or a circular saw.

Once you've assembled the jig, run the router along the straight edge of the fence to create a matching straight edge on the base. To use the jig, clamp it at both ends of the workpiece with the edge of the jig aligned

with the desired cut. As the router rides along the jig, it leaves a perfectly straight, clean cut.

Cut dadoes at any angle

I reach for the dado-cutting jig when I have to cut multiple parallel dadoes on a panel. Most of the time these grooves are perpendicular to the short fence of the jig, but they can be cut at different angles. Like the straight-edge jig, this one needs to be clamped at both ends during use. As long as you use the same size bit each time and the

Straight-edge jig

Always use the same diameter router bit with this jig. A smaller bit will cut wide of the jig's edge, while a larger bit will eat into the jig.

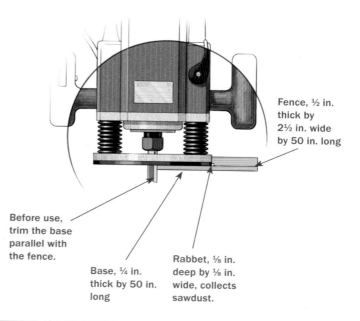

Fence, ½ in. thick by 2½ in. wide by 50 in. long

Before use, trim the base parallel with the fence.

Base, ¼ in. thick by 50 in. long

Rabbet, ⅛ in. deep by ⅛ in. wide, collects sawdust.

Straighten edges. Rough-cut the panel, then clean up the cut with this straight-edge jig.

Dado-cutting jig

Align the notch cut by the router in the short fence with the desired dado location.

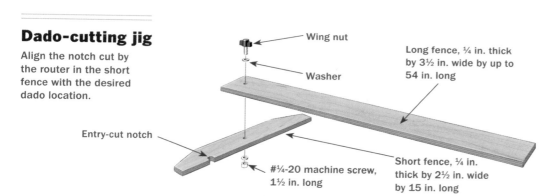

Wing nut

Washer

Long fence, ¼ in. thick by 3½ in. wide by up to 54 in. long

Entry-cut notch

#¼-20 machine screw, 1½ in. long

Short fence, ¼ in. thick by 2½ in. wide by 15 in. long

Variable-angle jig. Although dadoes usually are perpendicular to the long edges of a panel, this jig can make cuts at other angles.

Cut clean and accurate dadoes. Clamp the dado jig at both ends and make the cut in two or three passes.

Flush-cut edgebanding. This jig allows you to cleanly cut solid-wood edgebanding flush with the plywood panel.

Edgeband trimming jig

The router bit should be positioned a hair above the plywood surface. The spacer/guide block is clamped to the jig to steer the router along the edging.

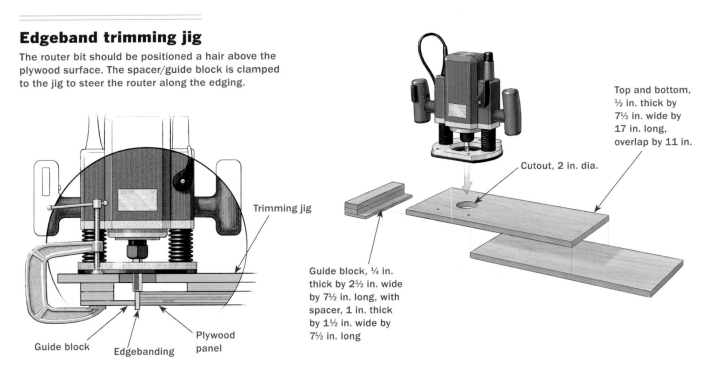

Trimming jig

Guide block

Edgebanding

Plywood panel

Top and bottom, ½ in. thick by 7½ in. wide by 17 in. long, overlap by 11 in.

Cutout, 2 in. dia.

Guide block, ¼ in. thick by 2½ in. wide by 7½ in. long, with spacer, 1 in. thick by 1½ in. wide by 7½ in. long

same angle, the entry cut on the jig's short fence will show the location of the dado. Use an up-cut spiral bit, which will prevent chips from jamming in the dado. For deep dadoes, make several passes.

Trim edgebanding quickly and cleanly

One of the hardest parts of using solid wood to edge plywood or laminate panels is trimming the edgebanding flush with the plywood. If you use a plane, you risk cutting through the thin plywood veneer, and sanding can leave cross-grain scratches on the plywood. The edgeband trimming jig enables you to trim the banding flush, quickly and flawlessly.

Mount the router on the jig, and set the depth of the bit so that it just clears the plywood surface. A router with micro-adjustment comes in handy. Adjust the guide block to align the bit so that the carbide tips extend just a hair over the plywood. Clamp the guide block tight, and you're ready to go.

Pay attention to the router bit's rotation and the direction you move the router. To avoid tearout, you want the leading edge of the bit to enter the wood first. Known as climb cutting, this method can be dangerous if the bit pulls the router forward uncontrollably. Because the amount of wood being removed is so small, you should be able to control the router easily.

Make turnings with a router

This turning jig allows you to "turn" round columns and posts using a router. To use the jig, first drill a ⁵⁄₁₆-in.-dia. hole, 1½ in. deep, in each end of the workpiece, then insert a steel rod to hold the workpiece inside the jig. Lock a drill stop on each end of the rod where it enters the jig to prevent the workpiece from shifting during the turning.

Clamp two wood guide pieces to the edges of the router subbase to restrict the router's side-to-side movement.

Turn on the router, slowly plunge down, and move the router halfway up and down the jig as you slowly rotate the workpiece. As you increase the depth of cut, you'll create a cylinder. Then repeat the process on the other half of the workpiece. Throughout the process, make small cuts for a better finish and a safer operation.

You can adapt this jig to create different turnings. Offset the hole at one end of the jig to make tapered turnings, or clamp blocks to the long sides of the jig to produce stopped turnings. If you design the jig with gently curving sides, the workpiece will become football shaped as it is turned.

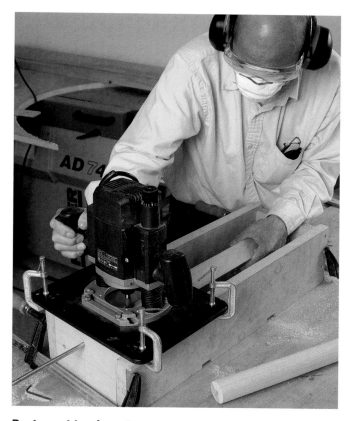

Router-cut turnings. By guiding the router back and forth while turning the workpiece, a square blank gradually becomes a cylinder.

Tapered turnings. Lower the hole at one end of the jig to taper the turned workpiece.

Stopped turnings. Clamp blocks to the side of the jig to leave a square section on the turning.

Turning jig

The dimensions of this jig will vary based on the size of the blank to be turned. The four sides of the jig can be screwed together or clamped for greater flexibility. Steel rods passing through each end of the jig hold the blank.

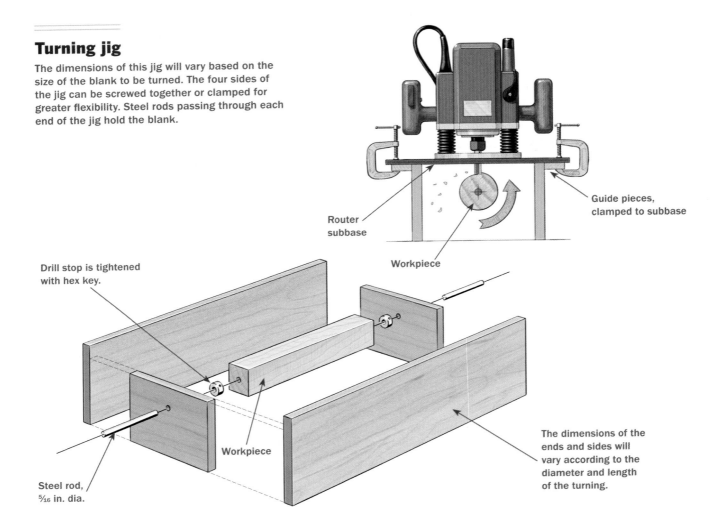

Guide pieces, clamped to subbase

Router subbase

Workpiece

Drill stop is tightened with hex key.

Workpiece

Steel rod, ⁵⁄₁₆ in. dia.

The dimensions of the ends and sides will vary according to the diameter and length of the turning.

Versatile Mortising Jig

MICHAEL C. FORTUNE

One of the challenges when working with curved parts is how to cut joinery on them. When tapering solid stock, it's best to cut the joinery before cutting the taper, but this is not possible with laminated work. A few years back, I created a simple jig that enables me to cut mortises in a variety of curved pieces. I've since discovered that the jig works equally well when mortising straight pieces, or cutting mortises in end grain.

The jig consists of a mounting block, a fixed vertical piece, and a sliding top surface. The mounting block is secured to the front edge of a workbench between two benchdogs. Alternatively, it can be screwed to a longer piece of plywood that is clamped to the top of the workbench.

It is important that the dadoes in the top surface and the mounting block are in matching locations to receive the ¾-in.-thick ultrahigh molecular weight (UHMW) plastic slide bars. The plastic and other hardware is available at www.rockler.com.

Lay out the mortise on the workpiece and then clamp it to the front vertical surface of the jig, touching the underside of the top. Now slide the top forward until the mortise is centered in the large viewing slot. Eyeballing it is sufficient, as once set up, the jig will cut matching parts identically. Now place the router on the jig and lower the bit until it just touches one end of the mortise. Slide the adjustable stop up to the base

(round or square) of the router and tighten the wing nut. Repeat these steps at the other end.

Although you can use any straight bit, I use two-flute (three- or four-flute bits won't plunge) high-speed end mills available at www.wttool.com. You will need to buy a collet adapter for the ⅜-in.-dia. shaft. The bits work perfectly at 12,000 rpm to 20,000 rpm. I plunge in a maximum ⅛ in. and do a medium-fast pass from side to side, not hesitating at the ends. The bit's spiral upcut design clears the chips from the mortise and a vacuum attached to the router removes them.

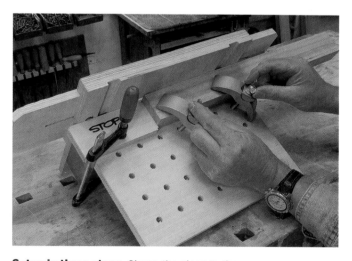

Setup in three steps. Clamp the piece to the jig. Center the mortise in the viewing port and tighten the hold-down clamps. If more than one piece is being cut, a stop block aids repeatability.

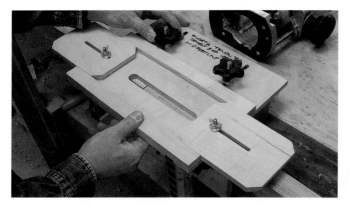

Adjust front to back and side to side. Slide the top so the view port is centered on the mortise (above). With the router bit just touching one end of the mortise (right), move the slide until it touches the router base and tighten the wing nut.

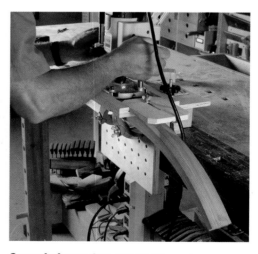

Mortise three ways. On straight pieces, with the workpiece secure and the jig aligned, use a straight-cutting bit to excavate the mortise, increasing the depth ⅛ in. with each pass. You can either square up the mortise with a chisel or use a rounded loose tenon.

Stop, plywood, ½ in. thick by 6 in. long, same width as the router base

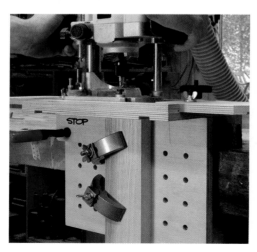

Into end grain. The jig is flexible enough to allow end-grain mortises to be cut, such as for slip tenons.

Curved pieces, too. The jig allows clean, accurate mortises to be cut on all sorts of curved pieces.

Mortising jig

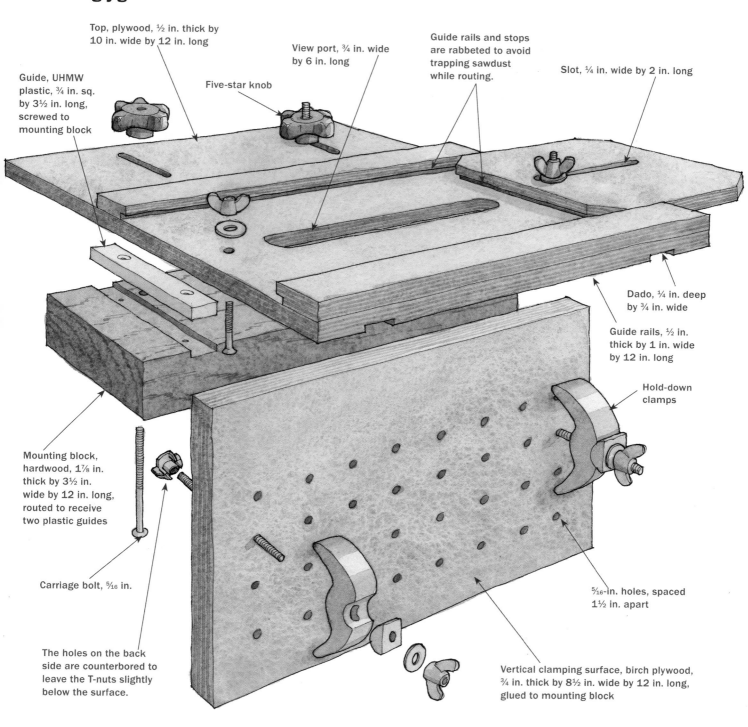

Top, plywood, ½ in. thick by 10 in. wide by 12 in. long

View port, ¾ in. wide by 6 in. long

Guide rails and stops are rabbeted to avoid trapping sawdust while routing.

Slot, ¼ in. wide by 2 in. long

Guide, UHMW plastic, ¾ in. sq. by 3½ in. long, screwed to mounting block

Five-star knob

Dado, ¼ in. deep by ¾ in. wide

Guide rails, ½ in. thick by 1 in. wide by 12 in. long

Hold-down clamps

Mounting block, hardwood, 1⅞ in. thick by 3½ in. wide by 12 in. long, routed to receive two plastic guides

Carriage bolt, ⁵⁄₁₆ in.

The holes on the back side are counterbored to leave the T-nuts slightly below the surface.

⁵⁄₁₆-in. holes, spaced 1½ in. apart

Vertical clamping surface, birch plywood, ¾ in. thick by 8½ in. wide by 12 in. long, glued to mounting block

Templates Guide the Way

DOUG PETERMAN

When the talk turned to tools at a recent woodworkers' meeting, I surprised myself by naming router templates as my favorite. Don't get me wrong: I love hand tools and use them constantly, but my work would be less efficient and less profitable without these simple but versatile templates.

Router templates can be used to create and fine-tune furniture forms before cutting into expensive stock. They allow me to see a design full-size and in relation to the other parts of a piece. Not to mention, templates make it easy to reproduce identical parts.

Almost all template-routing operations require only a handful of tools, including a router, two common bearing-guided bits, a bandsaw, a sander, and a shopmade template. With those items and a few drawing tools, such as a compass or even french curves, you are fully equipped to tackle any template-routing job.

Making a template

Templates can be made from any stiff sheet material with enough strength and thickness to guide the bearing on a router bit. In a pinch, I've even used scrap wall paneling and old crate lumber, but there are better choices. Mainly, I use two materials: ⅛-in.-thick Masonite for one-offs and ¼-in.-thick Baltic-birch plywood for production. Both have the basic characteristics of dimensional stability and consistency (no hard or soft spots) and are readily available.

Drawing the pattern

Trusting your eye is the quickest route to getting the shape you want in a template, but drawing tools will help you get there.

Making a template for routing

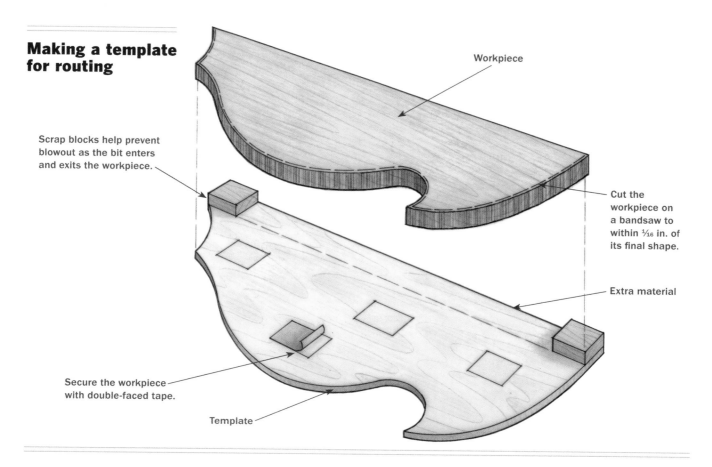

Workpiece

Scrap blocks help prevent blowout as the bit enters and exits the workpiece.

Cut the workpiece on a bandsaw to within ⅟₁₆ in. of its final shape.

Extra material

Secure the workpiece with double-faced tape.

Template

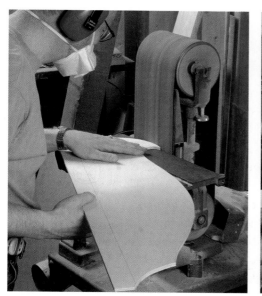

Glue scrap blocks to the template. The blocks prevent the bit from catching the corner of the workpiece and damaging it upon exit and entry.

Cut and sand the template. After roughing out the template on the bandsaw—cutting ⅟₁₆ in. outside the line—smooth the template to its final shape using a belt sander (left) for flat or convex areas and a drum sander (right) for inside curves. Subtle irregularities are difficult to see, so inspect your template for dips and bumps by running your hand across its edge.

Begin with the template on the bottom

With the template on the underside of the workpiece, use the pattern bit to rout all of the areas where the bit is cutting in the same direction as the grain. Leave the remaining areas uncut.

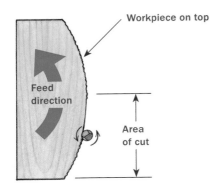

Workpiece on top

Feed direction

Area of cut

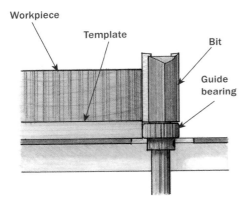

Workpiece

Template

Bit

Guide bearing

Template-routing. To avoid tearout when the grain changes direction on a workpiece, flip the piece onto its opposite side to reverse the direction of the cut. At the same time, switch from a pattern bit to a flush-trimming bit instead of removing the template and remounting it on the other side.

I usually begin by sketching the template pattern directly on the surface of the workpiece, especially when I'm working to preserve the grain in a particular board. Once I'm satisfied with the shape, I transfer it to the template stock.

When drawing the pattern on the template, it's a good idea to add at least 1 in. of material lead-in and exit beyond the workpiece edge wherever possible. Without

it, the bit can catch as you try to make the first corner of the template meet the bearing. Believe me, I've done it.

Whether you draw a pattern freehand or with drawing tools, you often will be left with bumpy lines and rough transitions that need to be smoothed out. The trick to achieving a smooth, or fair, curve is to get your eyes right down near the drawing surface and look along the line. Bumps

Flip the workpiece and change the bit

With the template on top of the workpiece, use the flush-trimming bit to rout the remaining areas in the opposite direction.

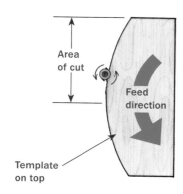

Area of cut

Feed direction

Template on top

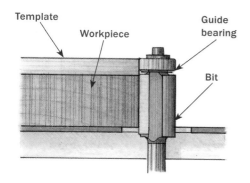

Template

Workpiece

Guide bearing

Bit

and dips are easy to see, but also look for transitions that are too abrupt. Work your way along the line, refining it until the curves are fair.

Rough-cut on the bandsaw, then sand

When rough-cutting the template, keep the blade about 1/16 in. from the pencil line to leave enough stock for sanding and final smoothing.

To get to the final shape, use a stationary belt sander. I use two—a 6-in. belt and a 1-in. belt—and both run with the table perpendicular to the vertical belt. For tight inside curves, a sanding drum mounted in the drill press is ideal.

Power sanding to a line involves a few simple rules. First, keep the material moving smoothly with even speed and light pressure. Never let it stop. Second, for optimal control, try to have the waste come off so that you hit the line just as the template passes the trailing edge of the belt or the center of the drum. This gives you one spot to watch and the comfort that the rest of the abrasive belt is safely cutting waste. Finally, work on bumps and dips by sanding the areas around them. Start before the fault, sand smoothly through it, and carry on a bit beyond.

If you don't have power-sanding equipment, templates can be smoothed by hand, using either files or sandpaper. I prefer files because it's easier to keep a square edge with them. Use a flat file along the edge on convex curves and a half-round or round file pointed diagonally across the template but still moving along the edge for concave areas. Sand as the last step if you must, but use a very firm or hard block to avoid rounding the edge.

To check your work, slide your hand over the finished piece to find any bumps or dips. Smooth them out as needed.

Using the router templates

When routing a workpiece with a template, I use bearing-guided straight bits (known as flush-trimming bits) when the bearing is on the tip and pattern or template bits when the bearing is on the shank. You need one of each type; mine are ½-in. bits with a cutter length of 1 in. When using these straight bits with templates that are exactly the size of the finished piece, there's no need to add offset for a bushing and no worries that a bushing may be off center.

The bearings should be exactly the same diameter as the cutter path to produce a flush cut. A good way to test is to make one pass with only the bit riding on the template edge; then make a second pass with the bearing riding on the surface that was just cut.

There should be no step between the first cut and the second cut. If the bearing has left an impression where it rolled along the cut surface, it means your router has excessive runout, you have a bad bearing, or the bit does not run true. In all of these cases, the bearing is acting like a hammer as it swings around just off the center of rotation.

Secure the template to the workpiece

For quick one-off routing, attach a template with double-faced tape or a few globs of hot-melt glue.

If I have to make several parts with the same template, I try to use clamps (shopmade cams, wing nuts or knobs, toggle clamps, etc.) to hold the work. Vacuum clamping works well for production pieces where you need 360° access to the piece. Special needs call for creativity: Templates can be made into two-sided jigs or jigs that box in a piece—anything to get the template securely in place.

Trim the waste on the bandsaw

With the template attached to the workpiece, use a bandsaw to cut away the bulk of the waste. Cut to about ¹⁄₁₆ in. from the line all around to reduce routing time. I used to leave more wood and hog it off with the router, but those heavy cuts sometimes raised chips that ran into the grain below the template edge. For quick trimming—especially handy when producing multiple copies of a template—I attach a finger guide to the bandsaw tabletop to keep the template ¹⁄₁₆ in. from the bandsaw blade. This also ensures that the cut stays on the waste side of the workpiece.

Use a router table and two straight bits

I do as much template routing as possible on the router table. Only when the workpiece is too large to be coaxed across the table will I take the router to the piece. Setup is very simple: Just mount the bit and raise or lower it until the bearing is lined up with the template.

Troubleshooting common problems

BUMPS

Bumps occur when the template loses contact with the bearing. This often is caused by chips impairing the edge of the template. Also, make sure the bearing is running

against the template and not the workpiece, and then take another pass.

DIPS

If the router bit slips, the bearing will lose contact with the template, and the cutter will dig into the workpiece. To avoid this

tough-to-repair mistake, make sure the router-bit height is locked securely, and keep steady pressure on the workpiece while cutting.

TEAROUT

Tearout results from cutting against the grain, when the bit lifts fibers and breaks off small chips. Routing with the grain is the simplest solution. When routing highly

figured wood, you can avoid tearout by changing the cutting direction more frequently.

BURNING

Burn marks are left when the workpiece moves too slowly past the bit; they show up worst on end grain. To avoid burning the finished edge,

move the workpiece more quickly past the bit for the final pass.

As much as possible, rout with the grain. If you think of the grain as a stack of paper, the cutter should be making the edge of each sheet lie down, not lift up. This is why you need both types of bearing-guided router bits. To rout with the grain on all edges of the workpiece, you must flip over the workpiece and alternate between the two bearing-guided router bits.

One thing to avoid is climb cutting, which is when the bit is spinning in the same direction as the workpiece is being fed. This is dangerous and should be attempted only where almost all of the waste has been trimmed off. Even so, always anticipate the workpiece being pulled forward into the cut, and keep your hands out of the bit's path.

Starting with the pattern bit in a router table, rout all of the areas that you can without lifting the grain. Change to the flush-trimming bit, flip the workpiece so that the template is on top, and rout the remaining uncut areas, going with the grain. If you have trouble keeping track of grain direction, draw arrows on the worksurface that point in the direction of the grain.

A Guide to Guide Bushings

GREGORY PAOLINI

Better than bearings. The advantage of a guide bushing is that it stays fixed and stable against its reference surface while allowing the bit to spin and plunge freely.

Routers need guidance, something firm and fixed to make sure the bit goes only where you want it to. Think bearing-guided bits, edge guides, and fences.

But there's a type of guide that woodworkers often overlook: the guide bushing. It's often the simplest, fastest way to make accurate and repeatable cuts—some of them difficult or impossible with any other type of guide. Used with simple shopmade templates, bushings make it easy to cut mortises, bore dowel and shelf-pin holes, and rout evenly spaced stopped dadoes in a carcase.

Bushings have several unique strengths. They allow you to plunge-cut and use spiral bits, which aren't available with bearings. You can cut into the middle of a workpiece, not just along its edge. And you never have to worry about a bearing wearing out and seizing up during a cut or burnishing the edge of the work.

The bit to use. You can use a bushing with nearly any router bit, but a spiral upcutting bit works best for most cuts.

Don't forget the offset

The most important thing to learn about using bushings is the offset—the distance between the cutting edge of the router bit and the outside edge of the bushing. The offset is the key to creating jigs and templates to cut the sizes and shapes you want. To determine the offset, subtract the bit diameter from the bushing diameter and divide by two. For example, with a ¾-in.-dia. bushing and a ½-in.-dia. bit, the difference is ¼ in. Half that, or ⅛ in., is the offset, so the edge of the template must be ⅛ in. from the edge of the cut.

Second, be sure the offset is large enough for chips to exit the cut. That's critical if you use a spiral upcutting bit to cut mortises. The bit helps clear out chips that inevitably build up and pack the slot, but you have to give the chips somewhere to go. I like to use a bushing with a ½-in. or ⅝-in. outside diameter and a ¼-in.-dia. bit.

Third, be sure the bushing isn't longer than your template is thick. Otherwise, the bushing will hit the workpiece and you'll be dead in the water. Either make the template out of thicker material or trim the bushing as shown on p. 124.

The other key is that the bit and guide bushing are very close to concentric; otherwise, the offset will be greater on one side of the router than the other. That can produce a too-narrow mortise or a slot with a wavy edge. Some router manufacturers sell centering cones to help adjust the offset, but I use a simpler method (see "Setup Tips" on p. 124). To adjust the bushing location on most routers, you'll need to adjust the base. You may need to enlarge the mounting holes or replace the baseplate.

On the following pages are my favorite jigs and templates for guide bushings. You'll come up with many more.

TIP With a plunge router, if you go too deep, the spinning router collet will hit the guide bushing—and burning metal is an unpleasant aroma. So set the depth stop accordingly.

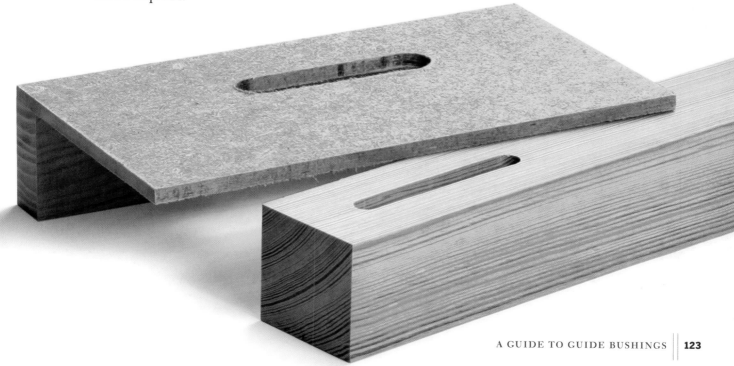

Setup Tips

THEY OFTEN NEED A TRIM

Too much of a good thing. Most bushings are too long for ¼-in.-thick template stock. As is, this one will hit the workpiece.

Easy to trim. Use a hacksaw to trim the bushing to just under the thickness of your template stock. Clean up the sawn edge with coarse sandpaper.

ALIGNMENT IS ESSENTIAL

Dovetail-bit test. To find out if the bushing and bit are concentric, raise a dovetail bit until it nearly touches the bushing, then spin it by hand. You'll quickly see if the bushing is off-center.

Tape marks the spot. Just in case the offset between the bit and the bushing is still a little inconsistent, Paolini keeps the router in the same relative position for each pass, ensuring a consistent cut. The piece of green tape is his reference.

Seven super jigs for bushings

These simple templates and patterns let you cut mortises, holes, slots, and elaborate shapes with a plunge router fitted with a guide bushing and a spiral upcutting bit. All the jigs begin with a piece of ¼-in.-thick plywood or MDF.

Mortising is job one

This simple jig lets you cut the same mortise on workpieces of different sizes. I have versions for common mortise sizes, and I just grab the one I need. The jig works on the sides and ends of a workpiece, so it's ideal for loose-tenon joinery.

Make the base as wide as your router's base and twice as long. Attach it to a hardwood fence milled flat and square. Lay out the

Mortising jig

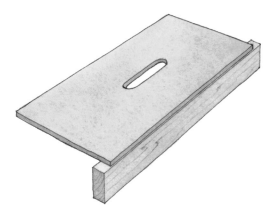

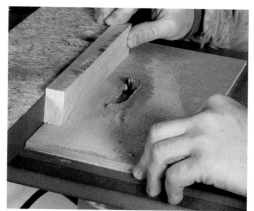

2. Slot the base. Hold the jig's fence against the router-table fence and carefully lower the template onto the bit to start the slot.

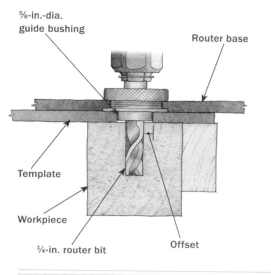

⅝-in.-dia. guide bushing

Router base

Template

Workpiece

¼-in. router bit

Offset

1. Attach the fence. Leave the fence slightly proud of the base so you can reference off it when cutting the slot for the bushing.

3. How to use the jig. Attach the jig using a vise (shown) or clamps. Make full-depth plunge cuts at the ends of the slot, with a series of shallower passes to clean out the middle. Blow out the chips before making a final pass. Don't forget to record the bushing size and bit size on the jig for future reference.

mortise slot on the bottom of the template, adding the proper offset to the width and length. Cut the slot at the router table, and try to make it fit the bushing exactly. If you have a bit that's the same size as the outside of the guide bushing, use it. Otherwise, use a smaller bit and cut the slot in multiple passes. Some people drill a starter hole for this kind of cut, but I find it unnecessary. I rest the right side of the template on the router table, then carefully lower the left side onto the spinning bit and move the template right to left to make the cut.

For workpieces of different thicknesses, add shims next to the fence.

Piercing template cuts any shape, anywhere

This template lets you cut a decorative design or a recess for an inlay anywhere on any workpiece. Just like mortising templates, you use a piercing template with a specific spiral bit and bushing so that the cutout you make is always the same size. I find that a ⅝-in.-dia. bushing allows good chip ejection around a ¼-in.-dia. bit.

Like the mortising template, this one has a fence that is proud of the base. However, be sure that the edges of the base are square to the fence. That's because you'll have to rotate the base against the router-table fence to cut the holes, and you want to be sure everything stays square. Again, be sure to consider the bushing/bearing offset when laying out the holes in the template. Make a plunge cut to pierce the base and begin cutting the template. Position the template on the workpiece with carpet tape, clamps, screws, or a fence.

Piercing template

Cut the pattern. Use a ¼-in. straight bit to cut the pattern in the template. In this case, rotate the template against the router-table fence as needed.

Cut the workpiece. To pierce a workpiece completely, make a series of progressively deeper cuts until the waste pieces drop free.

Full pattern

One template, multiple cuts. Paolini designed this template so he could make angled cuts for through-mortises as well as decorative curved cutouts on the ends of a book rack.

Make a full pattern for a furniture part

The pattern shown here illustrates how you can make one template for multiple cuts both on the edge and in the middle of a workpiece. I created this pattern to make the end pieces of an Arts and Crafts book rack. The angled slots make through-mortises for tenons on the ends of the shelves; the other shapes are for decorative cutouts. I made all the cuts with a ½-in.-dia. bushing and a ¼-in. bit. It takes time and a bit of math to lay out and cut the slots. But you end up with a pattern that is well suited to limited production runs.

Just align the edge of the pattern with the edge of the workpiece and clamp the two together.

Make your own shelf-pin jig

You can buy a commercial template for drilling shelf-pin holes, but it only takes five minutes to make your own. The router bit has to be the same diameter as the shelf pins,

typically ¼ in. I use that bit with a ⅜-in.-dia. bushing. When setting the router's depth stop, don't forget to factor in the thickness of the template.

I usually cut the template long enough to fit the side of the cabinet I'm drilling, but it will work for taller pieces, too. Just drill the end holes with a ¼-in. bit, then drill the remaining holes for the bushing. To drill a second set of holes, use a ¼-in. drill bit to align the template with the last shelf-pin hole you drilled.

Doweling jig solves joinery problems

Dowel joints are a great problem-solver, stepping in when traditional joints won't work. You can use this jig to drill dowel holes in mating pieces.

Make the base wide enough to support the router and long enough to hold the longest workpiece. I use the one shown on the next page to attach stretchers to the legs of a table.

Shelf-pin jig

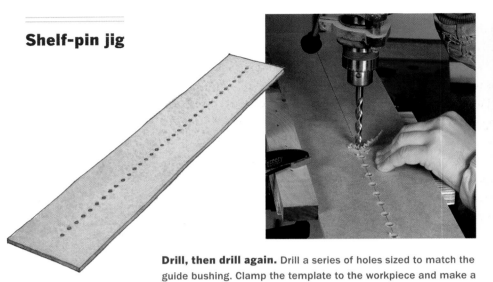

Drill, then drill again. Drill a series of holes sized to match the guide bushing. Clamp the template to the workpiece and make a series of shallow plunge cuts for the shelf-pin holes.

Doweling jig

Clamp the workpiece to the jig. The vertical fence and end blocks locate the legs. Paolini moves the stop block for the stretchers.

Flip the jig and make the holes. Use the router like a drill to plunge-cut the dowel holes.

Perfect fit. The jig ensures that the holes in the stretcher and leg line up perfectly. The joint is easy to glue up and very strong.

Drill holes to match the outside diameter of the bushing, centered on the workpiece and spaced as needed. As with the shelf-pin jig, the bit diameter has to match the dowel diameter. In this case, I used a ¼-in.-dia. bit and a ⅜-in.-dia. bushing.

It's easiest if both pieces are the same thickness. If they aren't (if you're doweling a thin apron to a thick leg, for example), make the jig for the thicker piece, then use shims to center the thinner workpiece on the template holes. If the ends of the joint don't align (as shown on p. 128), you can move the stop block or shim it.

Circle-cutting trammel

Cutting a perfect circle for a tabletop is a breeze if you use a guide bushing to position the router on a simple trammel—which is nothing more than a rectangle with holes in it.

Drill a pilot hole at one end for a screw that will be the circle's center point. From that center point, measure the desired radius plus half the router-bit diameter, and mark another center point. Drill a hole the same size as the outside diameter of the guide bushing you'll use. You can add more bushing holes to get several sizes of circle from one trammel. The size of the bit and bushing aren't critical. I normally use a ⅜-in.-dia. bit and a ⅝-in.-dia. bushing.

To make the circle, work on the underside of the workpiece. Anchor the center-point screw, slip the bushing into its hole, and make a series of shallow passes.

Parallel-groove jig

Use this jig to make evenly spaced long cuts, such as flutes in architectural elements or dadoes in the sides of a small cabinet (shown on p. 30). The jig requires only one setup—

Circle-cutting trammel

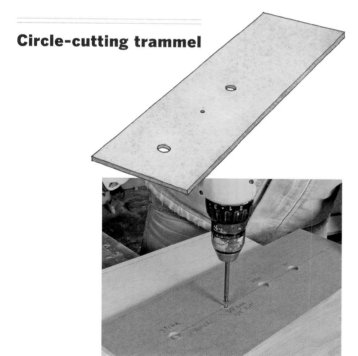

World's simplest trammel. A screw acts as the pivot point (in the underside of the stock), and the guide bushing drops into another hole. The bushing allows you to plunge the bit as you make progressively deeper cuts.

Parallel-groove jig

One setup, multiple grooves. Think of this template as a large router base that you slide along a fence. The series of holes for a guide bushing produces evenly spaced slots without having to move the fence.

you don't need to reset a fence for each new cut. And the jig allows you to make a series of stopped dadoes or grooves on the workpiece, which is tedious with a router and edge guide, and impossible with a tablesaw.

Unlike the other jigs shown here, this one is meant to slide along a fence rather than be clamped or pinned to the workpiece, so setup takes a couple of extra minutes. Make the jig wide enough that it will slide along the fence without tipping. Drill holes the same size as the outside diameter of the

guide bushing on the centers for the grooves you want to cut. For a ⅜-in.-dia. groove, I used a ⅝-in. bushing. Clamp a fence to the workpiece parallel to the desired grooves; if you're making stopped cuts, add blocks to set the beginning and end of the cuts. Butt the template against the fence, fit the router bushing into the first guide hole, and push the router along the fence to make the cut. Repeat until you have as many grooves as you need.

Climb Cutting: Don't Believe the Naysayers

CHRIS GOCHNOUR

Climb cutting sounds like an X Games sporting event, but there's nothing extreme about it. The technique, in which you move the router in the same direction that the bit wants to pull it, gets a bad rap as being unsafe. But it's a legitimate practice that every woodworker should use—in the right places.

The biggest benefit of climb cutting is that it prevents chipout and tearout when routing along an edge. For some cuts, it also lets you set the bit to cut full depth and just whittle away until you get close, a real time-saver.

Climb cutting is no more dangerous than any other machine technique. But to do it safely, you first need to understand when to do it and how the router will behave during the cut.

What makes the climb cut tricky

Many woodworking instructors tell their students they should always rout against the rotation of the bit, often called a push cut. Push cutting does provide maximum control over the tool, so it's considered safer and is the reason why beginners are taught to rout this way. But push cutting can cause the unsupported wood fibers ahead of the bit to tear out (see the drawing on p. 132). That's where climb cutting can help.

Climb cutting cuts the wood on the entry stroke, which compresses the wood fibers rather than lifting them. Each pass will be

Push cutting vs. climb cutting

In a push cut, the router is moved against the rotation of the bit. The counteracting forces make it easier to control the tool, but the technique is more prone to tearout. A climb cut eliminates tearout, but because the router moves in the same direction as the bit's rotation, the tool will want to take off on you.

A PUSH CUT IS EASIER TO CONTROL BUT PRONE TO TEAROUT

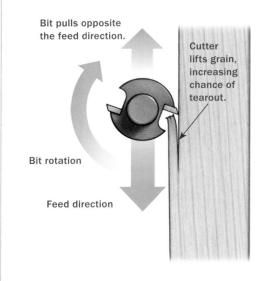

Bit pulls opposite the feed direction.

Cutter lifts grain, increasing chance of tearout.

Bit rotation

Feed direction

A CLIMB CUT IS TEAROUT-FREE BUT REQUIRES A FIRM GRIP

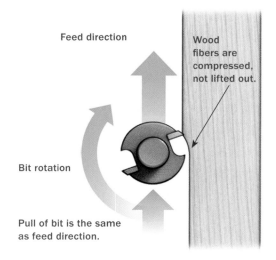

Feed direction

Wood fibers are compressed, not lifted out.

Bit rotation

Pull of bit is the same as feed direction.

tearout-free, but be careful. Climb cutting has more of a tendency to make the router "run" forward, so controlling the tool is job number one.

When climb cutting, use a broad, stable stance, like a boxer, holding the router firmly with both hands. Don't force the tool against the workpiece while climb cutting, because this will make the router take off on you. Instead, start the router and engage the workpiece with a light touch. Once the router contacts the workpiece, pull it toward you, using your arms to control the tool. When profiling, take multiple, light, controlled passes until you reach full depth.

In the following pages, I'll explain more about how to climb cut and when it's appropriate.

Rout perfect edge profiles

Large profiling bits are notorious for tearout. The solution is a climb cut. Set the bit to its full cutting depth and whittle away material. Finish with a push cut to eliminate any waves left by the climb cut.

Rough out mortises

When doing inlay or installing hinges, it's often easier to rough out the mortise with a router (see p. 136). In these cases, a push cut can be ruinous. With no bearing to anchor the bit, the router can stray beyond the layout line if you're not careful. For more precision, use a climb cut, which will push the bit away from the layout lines. When you get close, finish the mortise with chisels.

Joint veneer

To join pieces of veneer, you need crisp, straight edges that are hard to get on such fragile material (see p. 136). For the cleanest results, stack and squeeze the veneers between two pieces of ¾-in. MDF and joint the edges with a climb cut and bearing-guided bit. Make a final, light pass with a push cut.

Rout smooth curves

On most curves, whether concave or convex, the grain changes direction at some point, usually near the middle of the curve (see p. 137). So trying to rout the entire arc with a push cut will cause tearout when the grain reverses. The best approach is to combine a push cut and a climb cut.

When climb cutting is a no-no

NEVER WHEN TIED DOWN

Do not climb cut if the bit is trapped or tethered in some way and can't climb out of the cut, such as when using a circle-cutting jig.

NOT ON A ROUTER TABLE...

Use a push cut when feeding stock by hand. If you climb cut, the stock can be ripped from your hand, drawing your hand into the cutter.

...UNLESS YOU USE A JIG

If your workpiece is large, or locked into a heavy jig or sled, a climb cut on the router table can be made safely.

Edge profiles

CLIMB FIRST

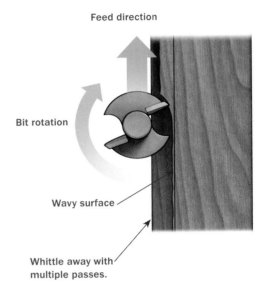

Feed direction

Bit rotation

Wavy surface

Whittle away with multiple passes.

Make waves. Climb cutting eliminates tearout, but it leaves a somewhat wavy surface in its wake.

PUSH LAST

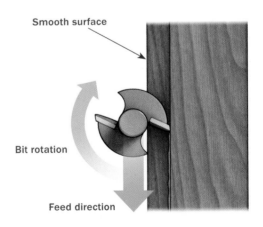

Smooth surface

Bit rotation

Feed direction

Calm the water. To clean up the wavy edge, make the last pass a light push cut.

CLIMB CUTTING ON PANELS: MOVE CLOCKWISE

With a handheld router, you generally move right to left to climb cut. On a panel, this means moving the router clockwise.

INSIDE FRAMES: GO COUNTERCLOCKWISE

Inside a frame, however, you need to move in the opposite direction.

Mortises

THE PROBLEM WITH A PUSH

Push cut can dive past layout lines.

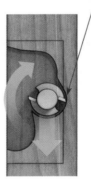

THE FIX IS TO CLIMB

Climb cut keeps you within the lines.

Veneer

STACK THE VENEER

¾-in. MDF

Top piece serves as a straightedge to guide the router.

Stack of veneer

Edges project from MDF.

¾-in. MDF

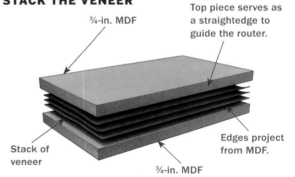

JOINT THE EDGES

Bit rotation

Feed direction

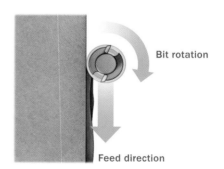

Curves

FIRST HALF

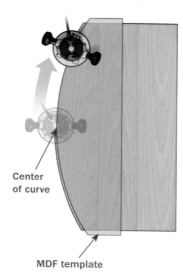

Center of curve

MDF template

DETAIL

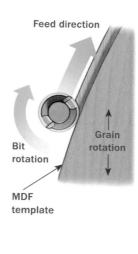

Feed direction

Bit rotation

MDF template

Grain rotation

Climb cut here. When routing the edge of a curved panel, say for a demilune tabletop or curved apron, use a climb cut on one half of the curve, starting near the top, or center, of the curve, where the grain is straight.

SECOND HALF

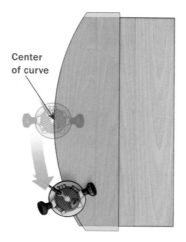

Center of curve

DETAIL

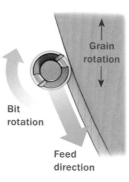

Grain rotation

Bit rotation

Feed direction

Push cut here. After climb cutting on one side, use a push cut on the other. As before, start the push cut at the center of the curve.

Eight Tips for Flawless Moldings

STEVE LATTA

A crisp molding lends the same touch of elegance to a well-made cabinet that a silk tie bestows on a sharp-dressed man. But in order for their magic to work, neckties and moldings both must be treated with care. A molding with torn-out grain or fuzzy edges will spoil the effect—like a soup stain in the middle of your chest.

I don't have to fuss with a necktie very often, but my students and I do run plenty of molding. I've adopted several techniques for making sure the results fit well and look their best. Creating molding safely and cleanly requires careful attention in three areas: cutting profiles, cleaning them up, and, finally, ripping the individual molding

strips. The suggestions here touch on all of these areas.

1. Use a sacrificial fence to tame tearout

To eliminate tearout, I like to bury the bit in a wooden fence, creating a zero-clearance cavity that lets the fence serve as a chipbreaker. There are two types of this fence that I make most often; both start with a good scrap of wide 2× stock with a jointed face and edge.

The first is a very simple fence that I make by using the bit itself to cut the zero-clearance cavity (see the drawing below). Clamp one end, bury the bit a little deeper than you need, then bring the fence back to the appropriate setting and clamp the free end. If you are raising the bit into the fence,

A simple fence for simple bits

A bit with no bearing or post on top can cut its own deep, zero-clearance cavity. Start with a jointed piece of 2× stock.

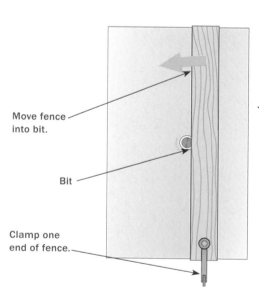

Move fence into bit.

Bit

Clamp one end of fence.

Bury the bit. Clamp one end of a wooden fence to the router table and, from the other end, carefully pivot the fence into the rotating bit. Then clamp it down.

A fence for complex profiles

Drilling the opening is easier for tall, complex profiles. To create zero clearance, bury the bit on the infeed side.

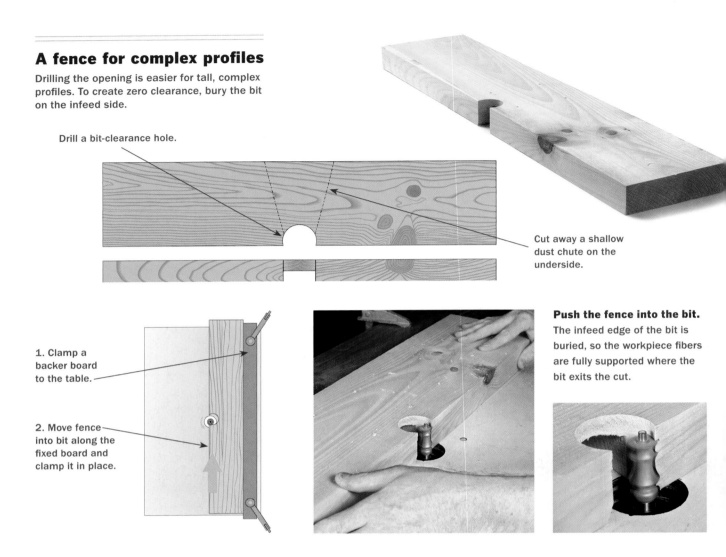

Drill a bit-clearance hole.

Cut away a shallow dust chute on the underside.

1. Clamp a backer board to the table.

2. Move fence into bit along the fixed board and clamp it in place.

Push the fence into the bit. The infeed edge of the bit is buried, so the workpiece fibers are fully supported where the bit exits the cut.

go only as high as necessary. Creating a cavity taller than your final bit height reduces the chipbreaking effectiveness.

For complex bits or those that can't cut their way into the fence, such as bearing-guided bits, I drill the fence opening with a Forstner bit (see the photos above). This also makes it easier for me to joint the infeed side if I need an offset fence. I also cut a channel in the back of the fence for chip removal.

To prevent chipout in heavily figured stock, I reorient this fence so that the bit is literally buried in the infeed side. To do this

safely, clamp a straight backer board behind the fence. Loosen the clamps that hold the fence and, with the router running, slide the infeed side of the fence into the bit. The movement is very controlled because the rotation of the bit pushes the fence against the backer board. After setting the fence, reclamp and continue running the molding.

Another advantage of any sacrificial wooden fence: I can quickly screw guards or hold-downs in place.

Of course, a good table and router are also important. Reinforce an MDF top with angle iron or C-channel, if need be, to prevent sag. As for routers, I recommend a fixed-base model with at least a 1½-hp motor.

2. Use the tablesaw to hog off waste

After drawing the profile on the end of a piece, I use the tablesaw to cut away as much waste material as I can, making sure the blade is tilting away from the fence (see the top right photo). Roughing away this extra stock allows lighter passes with the router.

3. Cut molding on a wide blank

Choose a piece of stock that is wide enough to run a profile on each edge while leaving a few inches in the middle. A bigger workpiece means less vibration and better results. It also lets you run the molding much more safely, keeping your hands well clear of the spinning bit while controlling the stock. It's also much easier to clean up moldings while they are part of a wider piece that can be clamped easily while the profile is scraped or sanded.

Pay close attention to the feed rate. Too fast leads to chipping; too slow can cause burns. Wax the table and fence to keep resistance to a minimum.

After the molding is done, rip it away on the tablesaw (see p. 147).

Keep fingers safe.
A wide workpiece can be fed into the cut with hands well clear of the bit.

Remove waste with tablesaw

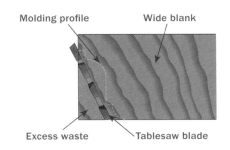

Molding profile   Wide blank

Excess waste   Tablesaw blade

Saw away the waste. Doing so saves wear on router, bits—and ears.

Create a thick blank from thinner stock

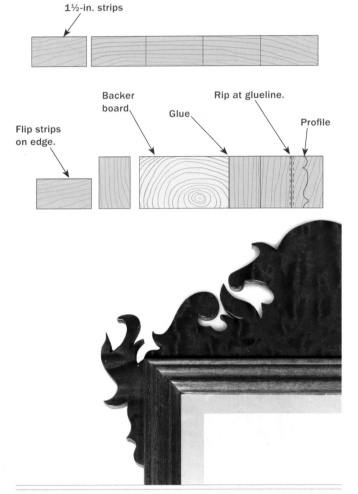

Cut from a wide board. This keeps your hands safe and, because a wide board is more stable, ensures that the work doesn't chatter as you cut.

Rip 1½-in. strips from 4/4 stock, flip the strips on edge, and glue them together, face to face. Use a scrap of jointed pine as a backer board in the center of the glue-up. After the glue is dry, surface the stock to the necessary thickness.

1½-in. strips

Flip strips on edge.

Backer board

Glue

Rip at glueline.

Profile

4. Glue up stock to produce a wide molding

When you want to cut a wide molding in figured wood like bird's-eye maple, you might not find stock thick enough. My solution is to make my own.

I do this by ripping a thinner board into strips a little wider than the thickness I want. Stand these strips on edge and laminate them face to face to create a glued-up board with enough thickness for the desired moldings. Glue up the blank with a piece of scrap stock as a backer board. This lets you cut multiple molding strips in the reoriented face grain while keeping your hands safely away from the bit.

Assemble the blank so that each glue joint falls in a tablesaw kerf when the moldings are ripped. You'll need to account for the kerf width, the amount of stock removed in cutting the profile, and the thickness of the finished molding.

5. Reduce chipout: Cut in the right sequence

Sometimes a simple profile requires multiple passes of the same bit. The simple cove shown at the top of the facing page is a case in point. Because I don't have a specific bit that cuts the proportions I need, I run this molding with multiple passes using a core-box bit.

In this situation, I find that I can reduce chipout dramatically by making the first pass with the bit set at the point farthest from the fence. I then raise the bit and move the fence toward the workpiece with each successive pass. In this way, the chipout created by each pass is removed by the subsequent passes. For the final run, I make sure the bit is buried in the fence, reducing the likelihood of any chipout.

This technique also helps when cutting complex profiles using a combination of different bits. This is sometimes necessary

Single-bit profile

Multiple runs with a core-box bit yield a custom cove. Each cut removes tearout from the previous pass.

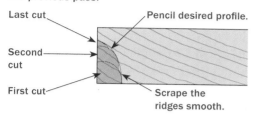

Last cut

Pencil desired profile.

Second cut

First cut

Scrape the ridges smooth.

Cover your tracks. When using multiple passes to cut different sections of the same profile, sequence the cuts so that each pass removes any tearout left by the previous cut.

Multiple-bit profile

Sequence the profiles to remove tearout, starting at the bottom and inside on the molding.

1. START ON THE INSIDE

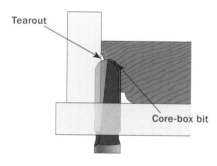

Waste cut on tablesaw

Drawn-in profile

Quarter-round bit

Tearout

Start with the lower quarter-round. Running this bit first will cause some tearout at its top edge. This line of tearout will be removed when the core-box bit establishes the cove.

2. THEN WORK IN THE MIDDLE

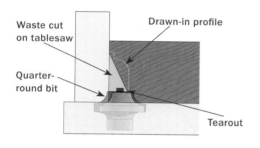

Tearout

Core-box bit

Run the cove in multiple passes. Raise the bit a little each time. Any chipout along the outside edge will be removed when the fillet is cut.

3. FINISH AT THE OUTERMOST PORTION OF THE MOLDING

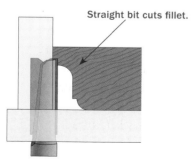

Straight bit cuts fillet.

Finish with the fillet. Use a straight bit buried in a fresh fence to prevent tearout.

because many complex-profile bits don't quite fit specific design requirements. By combining cutters, you can match older moldings or create original designs.

The delicate crown molding at the bottom of p. 143—for a small chest—is made by combining three cutters: an oversize beading bit from Eagle® America (www.eagleamerica.com), a core-box bit, and a straight bit.

Start by cutting a sample section of the profile to use as a setup piece. Creating this piece also brings to light any unforeseen problems in the process. If you create the molding often, hang the sample on the wall for future use.

6. Use an offset fence when molding an entire edge

Profiling an entire edge is very much like jointing the edge of a board: All of the original surface is removed to create the profile. With a standard setup, this means the profiled workpiece won't ride against the outfeed fence (see the drawing below). For proper support, the outfeed fence should be set flush with the cutter while the infeed

The problem: No outfeed support

No fence support. When the bit removes the entire bearing surface, a standard fence can't support the outfeed side.

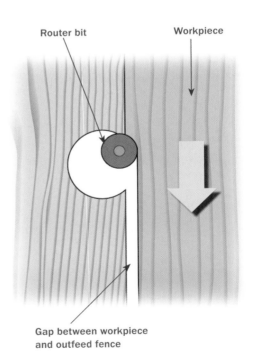

Router bit

Workpiece

Gap between workpiece and outfeed fence

fence steps in about 1/32 in. Make passes on a scrap piece to dial in the offset.

Although this might sound a little complicated, it's actually quite simple to set up. Take a jointed piece of 2× stock and drill an opening for the bit. Set the jointer to a 1/32 in. depth of cut and joint the edge of the fence just to the cutout. Lift it off the table and...shazam! You have an offset fence.

7. Clean up before ripping

Moldings generally need some cleanup, especially if the profile was generated by a combination of bits. Still, if the milling was executed properly, that cleanup should require minimal effort.

A variety of tools come into play for taking off tearout, tool marks, chatter, or burn marks. The list includes scrapers, a shoulder plane, files, and various sanding blocks.

Scrape first, using scrapers fashioned to a variety of profiles to fit the need (see the bottom left photo on p. 146). Shape cutoffs from card scrapers into an assortment of beads and rounds. For moldings like bracket feet, grind a scraper close to the profile. Don't

The solution: Make an offset fence

An offset fence in one easy step. Simply joint the infeed edge, stopping at the bit cutout.

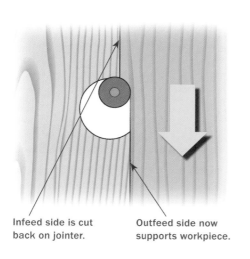

Infeed side is cut back on jointer.

Outfeed side now supports workpiece.

Running smoothly. The offset fence supports the work on the outfeed side and makes for a smooth cut.

go for an exact match because you'll need to attack from various angles.

Detail files work well for small radii and leave marks small enough to be removed quickly with sandpaper. Sanding, however, should always be kept to the essential minimum. I tell my students that after just a few minutes of sanding, the only thing they are really sanding away is their grade.

I tend to use aluminum-oxide paper ranging in grit from P150 to P220. Most times, I use a sanding block or a piece of dowel stock for an appropriate curve. Contour sanding grips are available, but these seem like one more thing I don't really need to accomplish a basic task.

This should be light duty. With proper cutting technique, moldings should need only minimal cleanup. Latta grinds custom shapes in card scraper stock.

Use a shoulder plane for flats and fillets. The Stanley® No. 92 works great at getting into corners.

Sand sparingly. Dowels of different diameters work well for coves and other hollows. Be careful to avoid rolling the dowel over any hard edges. Doing so takes away essential detail.

8. Rip between the blade and fence for consistency

When cutting molding from a blank, standard safety practice calls for setting the tablesaw fence so that the ripped molding falls to the outside of the blade. The fence is then reset and the process repeated for the molding on the other edge. But repeatedly resetting the fence can lead to variations in the thickness of the different pieces. This problem can make it harder to install the molding properly.

To avoid this, I rip off the molding between the blade and the fence. The distance between the fence and the blade never changes, so the thicknesses are far more consistent. And because you're not resetting the fence after each cut, the work also goes more quickly.

But this method demands extra precautions. Use a splitter to prevent the molding from curling into the back of the blade and causing kickback. Stub splitters stay out of the way but get the job done. Push sticks and hold-downs are also important. A small bandsaw cut in the end of the molding stock lets you hook a narrow push stick into it. A hold-down clamped to the fence keeps the stock from lifting off the table.

Rip to a consistent width. When ripping thin strips like this, a notch in the end of the stock provides a secure grip for a narrow push stick (right).

Taper Your Sliding Dovetails for Easier Assembly

MARTIN MILKOVITS

In my home, bookcases show up in every room, serving not only as places to store our growing collection of books, but also as places to display art and other items of interest. This bookcase is a versatile piece, big enough to hold a good number of books and/or collectibles while small enough to fit in almost any room.

The design is understated, with bracket feet and gentle curves along the tops of the sides, and maple back boards contrasting softly with butternut sides and shelves. The back boards are shiplapped to allow for wood movement.

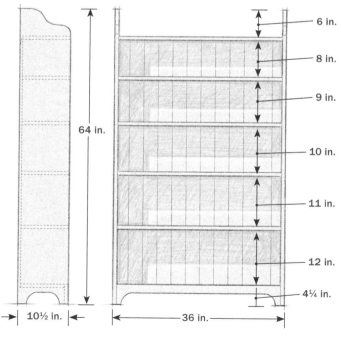

Anatomy of a sturdy bookcase

This butternut-and-maple bookcase can hold a heavy load of books. The tapered sliding dovetails that connect the shelves to the sides create a powerful wedged joint and eliminate the need for clamps during assembly. All of the parts are made of ¾-in.-thick stock, except for the back boards (see detail).

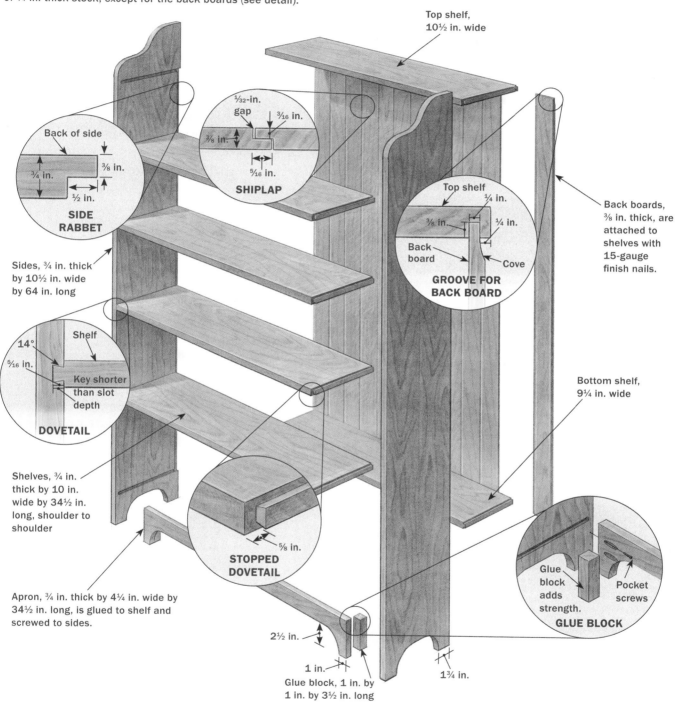

Top shelf, 10½ in. wide

SIDE RABBET

Back of side

¾ in.

⅜ in.

½ in.

SHIPLAP

1/32-in. gap

3/16 in.

⅜ in.

5/16 in.

Sides, ¾ in. thick by 10½ in. wide by 64 in. long

DOVETAIL

14°

5/16 in.

Shelf

Key shorter than slot depth

Shelves, ¾ in. thick by 10 in. wide by 34½ in. long, shoulder to shoulder

Apron, ¾ in. thick by 4¼ in. wide by 34½ in. long, is glued to shelf and screwed to sides.

STOPPED DOVETAIL

⅝ in.

GROOVE FOR BACK BOARD

Top shelf

¼ in.

⅜ in.

¼ in.

Back board

Cove

Back boards, ⅜ in. thick, are attached to shelves with 15-gauge finish nails.

Bottom shelf, 9¼ in. wide

GLUE BLOCK

Glue block adds strength.

Pocket screws

2½ in.

1 in.

Glue block, 1 in. by 1 in. by 3½ in. long

1¾ in.

Taper the slots in two steps

To ensure consistent results, the slots for each shelf are routed using a long fence and a plywood cleat. After the first pass, add a shim between the fence and cleat, then use the same router setup to taper the slot (see p. 152).

FIRST PASS

Attach a cleat to each case side. Screw the plywood cleat to the top of the inside case sides and perfectly square to the edges. Place screws in areas that will be wasted away when you profile the ends.

Clamp the fence to the workpiece. Align the front edge of the fence flush with the back of the case side and tight against the cleat at the top.

The shelves are attached to the sides with sliding dovetails, which are often used to connect cabinet tops to bottoms, to join vertical partitions to shelves, to attach molding to case sides, to connect breadboard ends to tabletops, and to attach drawer fronts to sides. Sliding dovetails provide a mechanical connection that will never pull apart. But that same quality also makes the joint difficult to assemble, especially with wide parts, so I taper the joint to make the glue-up go smoothly. In this case, I also stopped the dovetails for a clean look on the front of the piece.

Why taper the dovetail?

A sliding dovetail has two parts: the slot and the dovetail key. Here, the slots are routed into the case sides, and the keys are cut on the ends of the shelves. When you use this joint in wide stock, binding is a common headache during glue-up. The joint goes halfway home, then the glue makes the wood swell and the joint seizes. That's why I taper the joint slightly toward the front of the case. The taper—cut on one side of the slot and on the corresponding face of the key—makes it easy to slide the shelf in from the back without binding, and creates a wedging action in front as the shelf is tapped home.

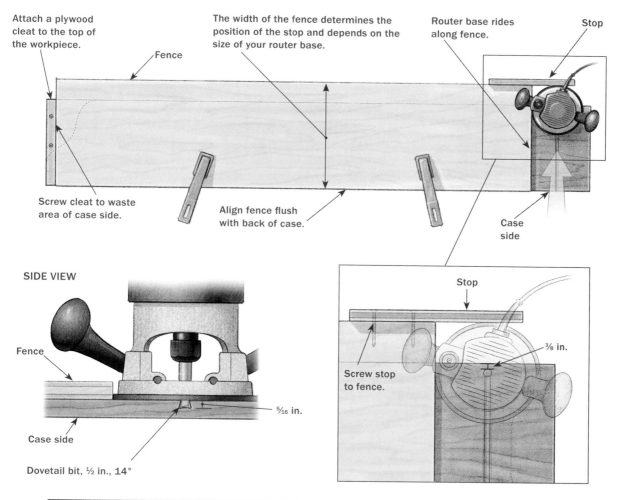

Attach a plywood cleat to the top of the workpiece.

Fence

The width of the fence determines the position of the stop and depends on the size of your router base.

Router base rides along fence.

Stop

Screw cleat to waste area of case side.

Align fence flush with back of case.

Case side

SIDE VIEW

Fence

Case side

Dovetail bit, ½ in., 14°

⁵⁄₁₆ in.

Stop

Screw stop to fence.

³⁄₈ in.

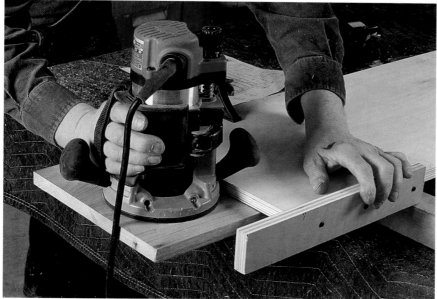

Rout the slot. Holding the router tight against the fence for control, cut until you reach the stop. Let the bit stop spinning before backing it out of the slot, or you could ruin the cut.

SECOND PASS

Shim out the back side. Place the shim between the fence and the cleat. Veneer tape is the perfect thickness (1/32 in.) to create the desired taper.

Reclamp and rerout. With the shim in place and the fence reclamped, run the router through the slot to add the taper.

Add a shim to taper the slots

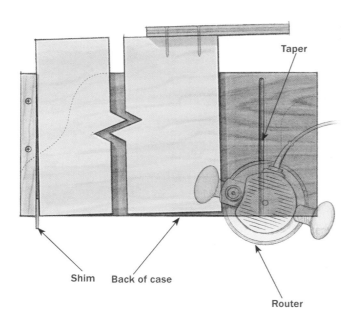

Taper

Shim   Back of case

Router

Trim the fence. After routing both slots for the bottom shelf, cut the fence down to repeat the process on the next set of slots.

The amount of taper is not that critical as long as it is consistent. I keep the taper to about 1/32 in. (about as thick as three business cards) per 10 in. of board width. With a taper like this, the joint can be almost completely assembled for trial fitting and can be driven home with a few mallet blows.

Router method simplifies complex joint

Tapered sliding dovetails can be cut by hand, using saws and chisels, but this method can be imprecise and time-consuming. I prefer to use a router and a few simple jigs to do the job. The method is clean and allows you to dial in the fit of each joint. To avoid confusion, be sure to label mating parts as you work.

Cut slots with a handheld router

For strength, the slot should be no deeper than half the thickness of the side. Likewise, the thin part of the key should be at least half the thickness of the shelf and the length at least one-third the thickness of the shelf.

First, screw a 3/4-in.-thick plywood cleat to the top of the case sides (see the left photo on p. 150). Mark the shelf locations on each side, then make a 3/4-in.-thick plywood fence to locate the slots in both sides. Cut the fence to a length that aligns the router bit with the lower shelf location, and rip it to a width that will place the router bit 3/8 in. from the front of the side. Screw a stop to the business end of the fence, and clamp the assembly in place (see the drawing on p. 151).

Set the router to make a 5/16-in.-deep cut and rout the slot across the side until you reach the stop (see the photo on p. 151). Next, remove the fence and place a shim between the rear edge of the cleat and the rear edge of the fence (see the drawing on the facing page). Reclamp the fence in place, then pass the router through the slot to create the taper along the bottom edge. Repeat this operation in the opposite side of the case. Once you have both slots for the bottom shelf routed and tapered, trim the fence to cut slots for the next higher shelf and repeat all of the previous steps.

Now is a good time to cut the bracket feet on the bottom of the sides, as well as the profile on top. Clean up those edges before proceeding.

Cut keys on the router table

Place the same bit you used to cut the slots into the router table, and set the depth so that it's a hair less (0.005 in. or so) than the depth of the slots. This will create a tiny gap to make the sliding action easier. Using a test piece the same thickness as the shelves, adjust the fence and take light cuts on both sides until the test piece fits about halfway or more into a slot with hand pressure (see the top left photo on p. 154). Once you've reached that point, you are ready to rout the actual shelves.

First, add a shim to the bottom rear of each shelf. The shim should be the same thickness as the shim used to taper the slots. Rout the top side of the key on each end of each shelf. Then flip each shelf to cut the bottom of the keys. At this point, each shelf should slide freely about halfway home but tight after that. To fit the shelves individually, make hairline passes across the top, straight side of each key until the shelf slides to within 1 1/2 in. of being fully home with only hand pressure (see the bottom photos on p. 154). Use a small, angled sanding block to dial in the fit.

Next, use a handsaw and a chisel to trim 5/8 in. from the front of the keys. Refine the fit with the sanding block if needed. Now rout a groove under the top shelf, 1/4 in. from the back edge, for the back boards. Next, rip the lower shelves to size along their back edges, and trim an additional 3/4 in. off the front of the bottom shelf to accommodate the apron. Finally, cut the rabbets that hold the back boards.

Taper the dovetail keys

Shim the rear edge of the shelf bottom and rout both sides of the shelf end.

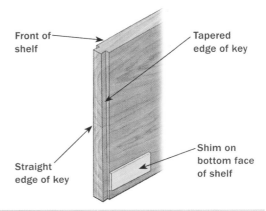

Front of shelf

Tapered edge of key

Straight edge of key

Shim on bottom face of shelf

Test piece gets you started. Take light passes along both edges of a test piece, made from a shelf offcut, until it slides halfway or more into a slot with hand pressure.

Shim out the bottom rear of the shelves. Use a shim of the same thickness used to taper the slots. Veneer tape is great because you can iron it on and take it off easily.

Fine-tune the fit. Keep making hairline passes on the router table to get the key to slide closer to home. To micro-adjust the fit, use a sanding block cut to the same angle as the dovetail bit and attach adhesive-backed P120-grit sandpaper to it (above left). The goal is to get the shelf to slide with just hand pressure until it is about 1½ in. from being fully home (above right).

Taper the keys. The keys are cut and tapered at the router table using the same bit that cut the slots, adjusted so that its height is a hair under the slot depth. Use a tall auxiliary fence to keep the long workpieces stable.

Glue in shelves, then add back boards

Once you have all the shelves fitted to the sides, the hardest work is done. Now's the time to glue up the case and cut and fit the back boards and apron (see the photos on p. 156).

The maple back boards are ripped to random widths no wider than 3½ in. Once the boards are cut to final size, use a raised-panel cove cutter to rout a ¼-in. tongue along their tops. Then rout the rabbets along their sides to create the shiplap.

To glue in the shelves, stand the sides rear-edge up on an assembly bench. Place a spot of glue inside the corresponding slots near the front edge, slide in the shelf as far as you can with hand pressure, then tap the shelf home with a mallet.

After installing the apron and glue blocks, the piece is ready for finishing (the back boards are finished before final installation). I sprayed on Deft® clear lacquer.

After you have the back boards in place, the bookcase is ready for your collection of Russian nesting dolls.

Trim ⅝ in. from the front of the key. Use a handsaw to remove most of the waste, and clean up the cut with a sharp chisel.

Assembly: No clamps required. Once the shelves are fitted, mill up the back boards and the apron. Cut the shelves at the back to their final widths, then cut the groove under the top shelf for the back boards. Finally, after you've rabbeted the sides for the back boards, you can break out the glue.

Push and pound. Stand the sides rear-edge up on an assembly bench. To install each shelf, place a spot of glue inside the corresponding slot near the front edge. Push in the shelf as far as you can by hand and fist, then rap the shelf home with a mallet. When installing the bottom shelf, put the apron in place to serve as a stop. Later you can screw the apron into place.

Nail in the back boards in order. Slide the top edges of the boards into the groove under the top shelf. To avoid misses, mark the shelf locations across the back, then nail each board to each shelf with 15-gauge finish nails.

Level Big Slabs in No Time Flat

NICK OFFERMAN

Nothing elicits greater gasps of delight from my clients than when I simply oil a piece of furniture and let the wood do the talking, in its velvety language of grain, figure, color, and magic. That's right, I said magic. You may think I'm waxing rhapsodic, but those woodworkers who have seen quilted figure jump out of a piece of newly oiled walnut know what I'm talking about.

It follows that wood will speak its magic the loudest when it is altered as little as

Ron Swanson. Nick Offerman plays the deadpan Ron Swanson in *Parks & Recreation* on NBC. Both Nick and Ron love breakfast meats, woodworking, and the great outdoors.

possible on its journey from inside the tree to underneath your dish of beef stew. Don't get me wrong, I love a Queen Anne highboy as much as the next pilgrim, but I also love to take a slab or block of wood, make it level and usable, put a hand-rubbed oil finish on it, and send it out into the world. Actually, I get my younger brother Matt to move those pieces. They are as heavy as heck.

How a farm boy became an actor became a woodworker

I grew up among a family of Illinois farmers (natural carpenters and mechanics), and despite my best efforts to escape this farm tradition with a career in break dancing,

I was ultimately forced to hang up my parachute pants. When I enrolled in the theater conservatory at the University of Illinois, my ambition far outreached my talent, and I found myself being cast in plays accordingly. My greatest role in college was the 92-year-old Ferapont, the butler in Chekhov's *Three Sisters*, with a grand total of three lines of dialogue. My saving grace was that, while all of the seasoned 20-year-olds from Chicago were masterful in their character work, they had literally never hammered a nail, let alone heard of a cordless drill. They could play the starring roles, but I could build the scenery!

My self-worth restored, I graduated, moved to Chicago, and found in my tool belt a way to earn dollars building scenery and props while acting in plays at night for peanuts. This arrangement made for an incredibly rich education in both acting and scenic carpentry. By the time I decided to leave for Los Angeles a few years later, I had my own modest scenery shop in a warehouse and a halfway decent resume of acting roles under my (tool) belt.

Live-edge coffee table

Shopmade leveling jig

The heart of the operation is a trough that guides the router over the workpiece. Extension wings are bolted on the ends, allowing 4 in. of up-and-down adjustability. Those wings ride on rails, which can be supported on a broad table, or a narrow workbench using support beams as shown. Except for its base, the trough is made from ¾-in.-thick birch plywood.

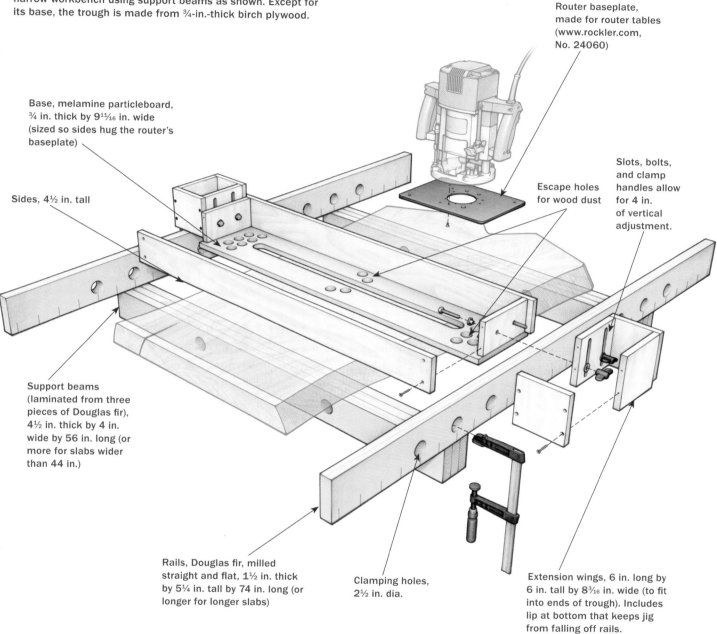

Router baseplate, made for router tables (www.rockler.com, No. 24060)

Base, melamine particleboard, ¾ in. thick by 9¹¹⁄₁₆ in. wide (sized so sides hug the router's baseplate)

Sides, 4½ in. tall

Escape holes for wood dust

Slots, bolts, and clamp handles allow for 4 in. of vertical adjustment.

Support beams (laminated from three pieces of Douglas fir), 4½ in. thick by 4 in. wide by 56 in. long (or more for slabs wider than 44 in.)

Rails, Douglas fir, milled straight and flat, 1½ in. thick by 5¼ in. tall by 74 in. long (or longer for longer slabs)

Clamping holes, 2½ in. dia.

Extension wings, 6 in. long by 6 in. tall by 8³⁄₁₆ in. wide (to fit into ends of trough). Includes lip at bottom that keeps jig from falling off rails.

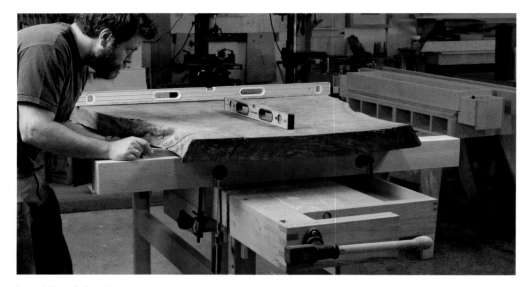

Level the slab. After leveling your workbench or worktable, clamp the support beams to it. Then the slab goes on and gets leveled. The idea is to even out the high or low points as much as possible to maximize the finished thickness. One long and one short level, plus a few shims, are all you need. Big workpieces like this will stay in place without clamps.

Upon arriving in Tinseltown, I was astonished to learn that Los Angeles has nowhere near the thriving theater scene that exists in Chicago. That meant no scenery dollars. Of course, the film and television industry require an enormous amount of scenery, but every shop I walked into was a union shop that wasn't interested in an aspiring actor. Lucky for me, one friend needed a deck, then another needed a cabin in the hills, which led to yet another post-and-beam folly in a west-L.A. backyard. Building these structures ignited my love affair with the chisel, as well as solid-wood joinery. As I studied the ins and outs of the mortise-and-tenon, I discovered books by George Nakashima, James Krenov, and Tage Frid (and, of course, *Fine Woodworking* magazine), and, before I could say "half-blind dovetail," I had a shop and my first clients.

The Nakashima bug

Like a lot of other woodworkers, I was enthralled with the designs of Nakashima, so I toured northern California to collect some tree slabs and began making what has

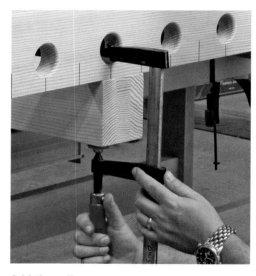

Add the rails. Size the jig and its support beams to accommodate the largest slabs you think you'll encounter.

become my shop's bread-and-butter item: the Nakashima-style dining table. The thing that sets a slab table apart from other popular furniture designs is the way the natural edge of the slab lends an organic yet elegant shape to the table. The tricky part is that

Adjust the height of the jig. The extension wings allow up-and-down adjustment, with guidelines on the ends to help you keep the jig level. Adjust the trough so it just clears the highest point of the slab.

chainsaw and portable sawmill cuts are often imprecise, and even well-sawn and properly dried slabs warp while they cure.

When I began making these tables, I used a power planer, a belt sander, and a couple of long straightedges to bring the surfaces flat within a tolerance of $\frac{1}{16}$ in., and then I sanded them for finish. Although this worked well, it was very time-consuming. I was beginning to accumulate orders for slab tables, as well as occasional tables that I make out of a large chunk of stump, so I needed to create a simple, convenient flattening system.

A router jig is born

It was a happy day when I came up with this versatile router jig. It was easy to build, and I'm still amazed at how quickly it levels a big, warped slab, leaving only a few minutes of sanding to do.

The heart of the operation is a bridge-like trough that guides the router on a level plane over the workpiece (see the drawing on p. 159).

Get your router ready. A rectangular baseplate (sold for router-table use) guides the router in the trough, and a wide plunge-cutting bit levels a 1¾-in.-wide strip with each pass. Offerman uses Amana Tool®'s A-Max No. 45453, 1¾-in.-dia. straight plunge bit.

Hit the high points first. Just slide the router along the trough to make a pass. One hand is enough to control it unless you hit a knot or other rough patch. Don't force the action. Make the final pass only about ¹⁄₁₆ in. deep for cleanest results.

Lining up a pass. Just slide the jig over, looking through the bit slot to see the edge of the last cut. You don't need to clamp the jig to the rails.

Tall sides prevent any sag across the span. The router is screwed to a router-table insert plate that keeps it steady in the trough. And the trough itself sits on rails, allowing it to be slid along the slab between passes of the router. That's it. Relatively simple but extremely effective.

I usually set everything up on my big tablesaw outfeed table, clamping the rails to a set of simple plywood towers. But for those of you who don't have a broad, flat table like that, I've devised an alternative rig that can rest on the floor, sawhorses, or any workbench. It works just as well. By the way, I recommend using a big plunge router.

How to flatten a slab

The first thing I do is take a close look at the rough slab and choose the side that will be the top. Usually that is the prettiest side, and the one without any rot. Then I seesaw the

Grip it and flip it. Tip the slab up on edge, and balance it there while you sweep the shims and dust off the rails. You might need some help. Then lay it down flat on its other side. Take a moment to enjoy how it lies perfectly flat on the support beams.

Rout the other side. You'll be surprised at how quickly the whole process goes, leaving smooth rows of router tracks on both sides of the slab.

Sanding goes quickly, too. Start with a belt sander, with 60-grit or 80-grit paper, and follow with a random-orbit sander, working up from 80 grit to 220 grit.

For a thicker slab, don't level the entire bottom

If the wood is very warped and would be too thin if flattened on both sides, I sometimes leave the bottom of the slab rough. I prefer the look of a thicker slab. Other times, a client wants the slab that way. The look does have a lot of character, but it doesn't leave a flat surface for attaching the trestle base. The jig offers a great solution. It lets me rout a couple of flat channels just big enough to accommodate the upper beams of my trestle base.

Place and trace the feet. Offerman leveled a smaller slab to make these feet. He decides where they will go on the underside of the tabletop, and then traces their location.

Flat spots for solid joinery

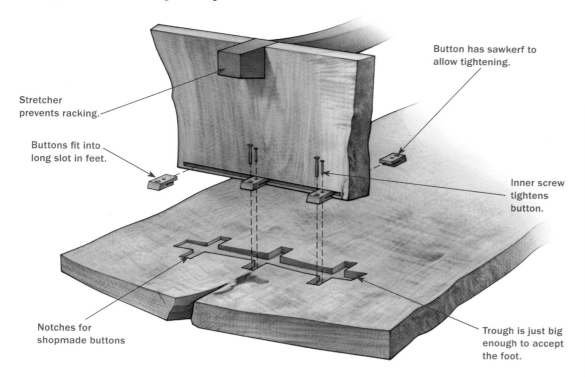

Stretcher prevents racking.

Buttons fit into long slot in feet.

Notches for shopmade buttons

Button has sawkerf to allow tightening.

Inner screw tightens button.

Trough is just big enough to accept the foot.

Lock the jig in place. A few clamps on the rails are necessary to keep the jig from sliding sideways, and a few passes get you to finished depth. Then move the jig over, lock it in place, cut to the same depth, and repeat until you've created a trough wide enough to accept the foot.

Room for joinery. Offerman uses a trim router to carve out extra landing pads for the buttons he uses to join the feet to the slab, squaring them up by hand with a chisel and mallet.

Don't forget the edges. Offerman uses a variety of tools, such as this "sanding star" drill attachment (www.woodcraft.com), to remove debris from the edges and prep them for finishing.

Just rewards. The first coat of linseed oil brings the claro walnut to life. Finish both sides equally to avoid warping.

slab up onto the base rails and use shims to even out the low points and high points as best I can (see the top photo on p. 160). The closer you can bring your high and low points to each other, the less material you will have to remove. Most of my slabs are so heavy that I don't have to worry about them shifting during the operation, but if you're working on a smaller piece, make sure your shims are secure and clamp down one edge of the slab.

I usually mill both sides of the slab if there's enough material to afford it. When you surface only one side of any piece of wood, it can react pretty drastically by cupping or warping, based on some fancy science reasons that I am not going to look up right now.

Offerman also uses his versatile jig to create beautiful side tables from stumps that would otherwise be thrown away.

Metric Equivalents

INCHES	CENTIMETERS	MILLIMETERS	INCHES	CENTIMETERS	MILLIMETERS
⅛	0.3	3	13	33.0	330
¼	0.6	6	14	35.6	356
⅜	1.0	10	15	38.1	381
½	1.3	13	16	40.6	406
⅝	1.6	16	17	43.2	432
¾	1.9	19	18	45.7	457
⅞	2.2	22	19	48.3	483
1	2.5	25	20	50.8	508
1¼	3.2	32	21	53.3	533
1½	3.8	38	22	55.9	559
1¾	4.4	44	23	58.4	584
2	5.1	51	24	61.0	610
2½	6.4	64	25	63.5	635
3	7.6	76	26	66.0	660
3½	8.9	89	27	68.6	686
4	10.2	102	28	71.7	717
4½	11.4	114	29	73.7	737
5	12.7	127	30	76.2	762
6	15.2	152	31	78.7	787
7	17.8	178	32	81.3	813
8	20.3	203	33	83.8	838
9	22.9	229	34	86.4	864
10	25.4	254	35	88.9	889
11	27.9	279	36	91.4	914
12	30.5	305			

Contributors

Yeung Chan divides his time between designing and building custom furniture and making hand tools based on his own ideas. He teaches at various woodworking schools, including the College of the Redwoods and Carleton College in Minnesota.

Michael C. Fortune, a *Fine Woodworking* contributing editor, has designed and built furniture for more than 30 years. He is one of Canada's most acclaimed contemporary furniture masters and was the first furniture maker to receive Canada's prestigious Bronfman Award for excellence in fine craft. He received the Award of Distinction from the Furniture Society in 2007. You can visit him online at www.michaelfortune.com.

Chris Gochnour, the owner of the Joiners Bench in Murray, Utah, has been building fine furniture for the past 20 years. He teaches furniture making at Salt Lake Community College, the Traditional Building Skills Institute at Snow College, and the Marc Adams School of Woodworking. Visit him online at www.chrisgochnour.com.

Steve Latta, a *Fine Woodworking* contributing editor, builds reproduction and contemporary furniture while teaching cabinetmaking at Thaddeus Stevens College of Technology in Lancaster, Pa. He lives in rural Pennsylvania with his wife, Elizabeth, and their three children, Fletcher, Sarah, and Grace.

Kevin McLaughlin is a mechanical designer and machinist by trade living in Helena, Ala.

Martin Milkovits, a furniture maker in Mason, N.H., is a member of the League of NH Craftsmen, Guild of New Hampshire Woodworkers, and the New Hampshire Furniture Masters Association. He has work on permanent exhibit in the Uncle Sam Museum in Sonoma, Calif.

Jeff Miller is a furniture designer, craftsman, teacher, and author of woodworking books and a frequent contributor to *Fine Woodworking* and other publications. Jeff's furniture has been shown in galleries and shows nationwide, and has won numerous awards. His furniture is in the Decorative Arts Collection of the Chicago History Museum. Visit him online at www.furnituremaking.com.

Nick Offerman is an actor, writer, and professional woodworker. He plays Ron Swanson in *Parks & Recreation* on NBC, but when the camera stops rolling, Nick heads for his L.A. woodworking shop, where he and his helpers turn out beautiful furniture from big slabs of distinctive wood.

Gregory Paolini owns and operates a custom furniture and cabinetry business near Asheville, N.C. He also writes and teaches about woodworking. You can see examples of his work at www.GregoryPaolini.com. In the past, he has reviewed tools for Festool, but he has not received compensation of any sort from the company.

Doug Peterman makes custom furniture in his home workshop in Stratford, Ont., Canada.

Gary Rogowski is the director of the woodworking school at the Northwest Woodworking Studio in Portland, Ore. He is a frequent contributor to several woodworking magazines and his latest book is called *The Complete Illustrated Guide to Joinery* (The Taunton Press, 2005).

Peter Schlebecker designs and makes furniture in Kensington, Md. He teaches at the Penland School of Crafts, the Woodworkers club in Rockville, Md., and occasionally at the Center for Furniture Craftsmanship in Rockport, Me.

John White, an experienced designer, cabinetmaker, and machinist, managed the *Fine Woodworking* woodshop for almost a decade. Now he splits his time between writing, teaching, designing, and consulting from his home in Rochester, Vt. You can reach him by email at zensmithvt@gmail.com.

Credits

All photos are courtesy of Fine Woodworking magazine (FWW) © The Taunton Press, Inc., except as noted below:

Front cover: main photo Andy Engel (FWW), left photos: Steve Scott (FWW). Back cover from top to bottom: Steve Scott (FWW), Anissa Kapsales (FWW), and Asa Christiana (FWW).

The articles in this book appeared in the following issues of Fine Woodworking:

pp. 4-11: How Many Routers Does Your Shop Need by Jeff Miller, issue 216. Photos by Steve Scott (FWW) except product shots by Michael Pekovich (FWW).

pp. 12-19: Tool Test: Trim Routers by Gregory Paolini, issue 220. Photos by Matt Kenney (FWW).

pp. 20-27: Tool Test: Heavy-Duty Plunge Routers by Gregory Paolini, issue 214. Photos by Matt Kenney (FWW).

pp. 28-39: Ten Essential Router Bits by Gary Rogowski, issue 186. Photos by Thomas McKenna (FWW) except photos of individual bits and boards by Kelly J. Dunton (FWW) and bottom two photos p. 30, top photos p. 35, top photo p. 38 and photo p. 39 by Michael Pekovich (FWW). Drawings by Christopher R. Mills (FWW).

pp. 40-49: Upgrade Your Router with Shop-Built Bases, issue 224. Photos by Steve Scott (FWW). Drawings by Vince Babak (FWW).

pp. 50-61: Router-Table Basics by Gary Rogowski, issue 190. Photos by Steve Scott (FWW). Drawings by Jim Richey (FWW).

pp. 62-70: A Versatile Router Table by Kevin McLaughlin, issue 169. Photos by Matt Berger (FWW). Drawings by Jim Richey (FWW).

pp. 71-77: Space-Saving Router Table by John White, issue 216. Photos by Matt Kenney (FWW). Drawings by Jim Richey (FWW).

pp. 78-89: Rock-Solid Router Table by J. Peter Schlebecker, issue 195. Photos by Anissa Kapsales (FWW). Drawings by Jim Richey (FWW).

pp. 90-95: Fundamentals: Handheld routing by Gary Rogowski, issue 194. Photos by Steve Scott (FWW). Drawings by Hayes Shanesy (FWW).

pp. 96-104: 5 Essential Jigs for the Router Table by Peter Schlebecker, issue 200. Photos by Anissa Kapsales (FWW) except photo top left p. 102 by Seth Deysach (FWW). Drawings by Vince Babak (FWW).

pp. 105-112: Five Smart Router Jigs by Yeung Chan, issue 177. Photos by Mark Schofield (FWW). Drawings by John Hartman (FWW).

pp. 113-115: Try This Versatile Mortising Jig by Michael C. Fortune, issue 197. Photos by Michael Fortune (FWW) except bottom right photo p. 114 by Steve Scott (FWW). Drawings by Jim Richey (FWW).

pp. 116-121: Templates Guide the Way by Doug Peterman, issue 170. Photos by Matt Berger (FWW). Drawings by Vince Babak (FWW).

pp. 122-130: A Guide to Guide Bushings by Gregory Paolini, issue 207. Photos by David Heim (FWW) except photos pp. 122-123 by John Tetreault (FWW). Drawings by Jim Richey (FWW).

pp. 131-137: Climb-Cutting: Don't Believe the Naysayers by Chris Gochnour, issue 220. Photos by Thomas McKenna (FWW) except photos p. 135 by Fine Woodworking magazine staff (FWW). Drawings by Christopher Mills (FWW).

pp. 138-147: 8 Tips for Flawless Moldings by Steve Latta, issue 197. Photos by Steve Stott (FWW) except individual board photos by Kelly J. Dunton (FWW) and bottom photo p. 142 by Mark Schofield (FWW). Drawings by Kelly J. Dunton (FWW).

pp. 148-156: Quick, Sturdy Bookcase by Martin Milkovits, issue 194. Photos by Thomas McKenna (FWW). Drawings by John Hartman (FWW).

pp. 157-166: Level Big Slabs in No Time Flat by Nick Offerman, issue 222. Photos by Asa Christian (FWW) except photo top p. 158 courtesy of NBC (©NBCUniversal Media, LLC), photo bottom p. 158 by Dean Della Ventura (FWW) and top left photo p. 166 by Rebecca Lee (FWW). Drawings by Christopher Mills (FWW).

Index

A

Amperage ratings, 92
Attachments, overhead, 67–69
Auxiliary fences, 101, 102, 103, 139–40

B

Bandsaws
    featherboards, 98
    sliding dovetails, 60
    template routing, 117, 119, 120
Base of router, 5, 6, 7, 19
    See also Sub-bases
Baseplates (router plates)
    for leveling jigs, 159, 161
    in router table construction, 66, 70, 73, 76, 81, 83, 84, 85–86
Bearing-guided straight bits, 38, 120
    See also Flush-trimming;
        Pattern/template-routing
        bits
Belt sanders, 119–20, 163
Bits, 28–39
    chamfer, 35, 53
    cove, 36, 37, 53
    dovetail, 34, 35, 59, 60
    flush-trimming, 38, 94–95, 118, 119, 120
    height adjustments, 14
    multiple-profile, 53
    panel-raising, 58, 60
    pattern-routing, 94–95, 100, 120
    plunge-cutting, 161
    profiling, 53
    rabbeted dovetail, 59, 60
    rabbeting, 32–33
    roundover, 36, 37, 53
    slot cutter, 34
    spiral, 32, 111, 122
    straight, 29–32, 54–57, 59, 60
Blowout. See Tearout
Bookcase project, 148–56
Bosch routers, 17, 24, 26
Bumps in workpiece, 121
Burning in workpiece, 92–93, 121
Bushings. See Guide bushings

C

Cambers, creating, 104
Carriages, adjustable, 62, 64, 65–66, 67, 70
Centering bases, 47–49
Chamfer bits, 35, 53
Chamfering edges, 35
Chipout. See Tearout
Circle-cutting jigs, 105–8

Circle-cutting trammels, 129
Circles, 106–7
Clamp blocks, 58, 65
Climb cutting, 131–37
    curves and, 133, 137
    for edge profiles, 132, 134
    for joining veneers, 133, 136
    mortises and, 132–33, 136
    on panels, 135
    push cutting vs., 131–32
    routing edge profiles, 132
    safety precautions for, 121, 131–32, 133
    technique for, 131–32
Coffee tables, 158
Collets, 92
Combination router kits, 5, 6, 7, 10–11, 90–92
Cove bits, 36, 37, 53, 142–44
Curved designs
    with mortising jigs, 113–15
    ogees as, 36, 37
    routing techniques for, 133, 137
    with template routing, 94–95
    wood grain and, 60–61, 133, 137

D

Dadoes, 30, 56–57
    bits for, 29–30
    dado-cutting jigs, 30, 108, 109, 111
    edge guides for, 93
    for panels, 108, 109, 111
    with parallel-groove jigs, 129–30
    stopped, 130
    See also Grooves, cutting
Decorative cuts and designs
    with cove bits, 37, 142–44
    with slot cutters, 34
    templates for, 126–27
    See also Edge profiles
DeWalt routers, 15, 16, 17, 27
Dining tables, 160–66
Dips in workpiece, 121
Dovetail bits, 34, 35, 59, 60
Dovetails, rabbeted, 59, 60
    See also Sliding dovetails
Doweling jigs, 127, 128, 129
Dowel joints, 127, 128
Dust collection, 72, 74, 76, 77, 88–89

E

Edgebanding, 13, 19, 38, 42, 110, 111
    See also Laminates, plastic;
        Veneers

Edge guides, 93–94
    See also Guide bushings
Edge profiles, 92–93
    bits for, 36–37, 53, 54, 90, 142
    climb/push cutting for, 132, 134
    complex, 142–44
    fences for, 139–40, 144–45
    for moldings, 54, 144–45
    multiple-bit profiles, 143
    for picture frames, 33
    single bit profiles, 143
    wide bases for, 41–42
Edges
    bases for profiling, 41–42
    bits for, 34, 37
    chamfering, 35
    finishing, 166
    jointing, 93–94
    trimming, 31
    veneers, 103–4, 133, 136
    See also Edge profiles

F

Featherboards, 54, 97, 98
Feed rate, 53
Fence guards, 69
Fences, 52–53
    assembling, 76–77
    auxiliary, 101, 102, 103, 139–40
    for cutting dadoes, 56
    modified, for dust collection, 72, 74
    offset, for moldings, 144–45
    parallel-groove jigs and, 129–30
    sacrificial, for moldings, 139–41
    for sliding dovetails, 59, 60, 151, 152, 153
    stopped cuts and, 58
    zero-clearance, 101, 102, 103, 139–40
    See also Fence guards
Festool
    plunge routers, 21, 22, 23, 24, 26, 27
    trim routers, 15, 16, 19
Fillets, 36, 37
Finger boards. See Featherboards
Fixed-base routers, 7, 10
Flush-trimming
    bases for, 19, 44–47
    bits for, 38, 94–95, 118, 119, 120
Forstner bits, 140
Furniture
    bookcase project, 148–56
    leveling slabs for, 159, 160–66

G

Grain of wood
    curves and, 61, 133
    panels and, 58
    template routing and, 100, 121
    See also Tearout, avoiding
Grizzly routers, 15, 16, 17
Grooves, cutting, 29–30, 57
    bits for, 29–30, 34
    fence attachments for, 92
    parallel-groove jigs for, 129–30
    See also Dadoes
Guide bushings, 122–30
    jigs for, 124–30
    Porter-Cable-style, 25, 26, 27
    setup tips for, 123–24

H

Handheld routers, 90–95
    dadoes and grooves with, 29–30
    edge profiles with, 90, 91, 92–93
    jigs for, 93–94
    for tapering dovetails, 153
    template routing with, 94–95
    tips for buying, 92
    vs. table mounted, 29
Height of router tables, 51
    See also Carriages, adjustable
Hitachi routers, 25, 26
Horsepower ratings, 11, 21, 92

I

Inlay work, 19

J

Jigs, 96–104, 124–30
    circle-cutting, 105–8
    dado-cutting, 30, 108, 109, 111
    doweling, 47–49, 127, 128, 129
    for edge trimming, 31, 110–11
    featherboards, 97, 98
    for handheld routers, 93–94
    leveling, 159, 160, 161–62
    miter angle sleds as, 102, 103
    mortising, 113–15, 124–26
    parallel-groove, 129–30
    pattern-routing, 38–39, 98–100, 127
    piercing template, 126
    shelf-pin, 127, 128
    straight-edge, 93–94, 108, 109
    turning, 111–12
    veneer, 103–4
    zero-clearance fences as, 101–2
    See also Templates
Joints and joinery. See Dadoes;
Dovetails, rabbeted; Dowel

joints; Grooves; Mortises, cutting; Rabbets; Sliding dovetails; Stopped cuts; Tenons; Veneers

K
Keys, 153–55

L
Laminates, plastic, 83, 84–85
Laminate trimmers. *See* Trim routers
Leveling jigs, 159, 160, 161–62

M
Makita routers, 17, 27
Masonite, 101
MDF (medium-density fiberboard)
    fences, 88
    jigs, 93–94, 99, 124
    router tabletops, 72, 76, 80–85
Melamine, 63, 64, 66
Miter angle sleds, 102, 103
Miter gauges, 55, 56, 63, 70
Miter tracks, 80, 81, 85–86
Moldings, 138–47
    chipout in, 142–44
    cleanup process, 145–46
    cutting process, 54, 141
    edge profiles of, 54, 144–45
    fences and, 139–41, 144–45, 147
    glueing, 142
Mortises, cutting
    centering bases for, 47–49
    climb cutting and, 132–33, 136
    jigs for, 113–15, 124–26
    spiral bits for, 32
Motor, 11, 21, 92
Multiple-profile bits, 53
Multiples
    cutting dadoes in, 30
    templates for, 127
    veneer-trimming jigs for, 103–4
    See also Template routing (pattern routing)

O
Offset, 123
    See also Guide bushings
Offset fences, 144–45
Ogee profiles, 36, 37
Overhead router carriages, 67

P
Panel-raising bits, 58, 60
Panels, cutting
    climb cutting, 135
    edgeband-trimming jigs for, 110–11
    straight-edge jigs for, 108, 109
Parallel-groove jigs, 129–30

Pattern routing. *See* Template routing (pattern routing)
Pattern/template-routing bits, 38, 94–95, 100, 120
Piercing templates, 126
Pin routing guides, 62, 68
Plastic laminates. *See* Laminates, plastic
Plunge bases, 6, 7, 19, 47–49
Plunge-cutting bits, 161
Plunge routers, heavy-duty, 20–27
    advantages of, 5, 7, 8, 9, 11
    bases for, 6, 7, 19, 47–49
    features, compared, 20–25
    manufacturers, compared, 26–27
Porter-Cable routers, 14, 15, 18, 21, 27
Profile cuts. *See* Edge profiles
Profiling bits, 132
Projects (bookcase), 148–56
Push cutting
    edge profiles and, 134
    vs. climb cutting, 131–32, 133

R
Rabbeted dovetails, 59, 60
Rabbeting bits, 32–33
Rabbets
    bits for, 32–33
    for router plates, 84, 85–86
    using dovetail bits, 59, 60
    using straight bits, 54–55
    See also Tenons
Ridgid routers, 14, 15, 16
Rock-solid router table
Roundover bits, 36, 37, 53
Router carriages, adjustable, 62, 64, 65–66, 67, 70
    See also Attachments, overhead
Router plates. *See* Baseplates
Routers
    features, compared, 15, 19, 20–25
    manufacturers, compared, 16–19, 26–27
    tips for buying, 92
    types of, 4–11
    See also specific types
Router tables, 50–61
    adjustable carriages, 62, 64, 65–66, 67, 70
    attachments, overhead, 67–69
    costs associated with, 66
    designs for, 62–70, 71–77, 78–89
    feed rate on, 51, 52–53
    height of, 51
    materials for, 66, 82–83
    plans for, 63–64, 72, 73, 80, 81, 87
    safety using, 53
    space-saving designs, 71–77

    tabletops, 66, 68, 69–70, 80, 81, 82–83
Ryobi routers, 14, 18

S
Safety, 53
    climb cutting and, 131–32, 133
    fence guards for, 69
    tablesaw precautions, 147
Sanders, 119–20, 163
Sanding
    moldings, 145–46
    slabs, 163
    templates, 117, 119–20
Shelf-pin jigs, 127, 128
Slabs for furniture, 157–66
Sleds
    miter angle, 102, 103
    for routing circles, 106–7
Sliding dovetails, 59, 60
    bits for 60, 34–35
    for bookcase project, 150
    drawer joints with, 59
    half-version (rabbeted dovetail), 59, 60
    tapering, 150–55
Slot cutter bits, 34
Slots, 153
Spindle locks, 9
Spiral bits, 32, 111, 122
Stand-alone routers
    advantages of, 8, 9
    compared, 16–19, 26–27
Stopped cuts, 58
Straight bits, 29, 38, 120
    See also Flush-trimming; Pattern/template-routing bits
Sub-bases, 19, 40–49

T
Table-mounted routers
    advantages of, 5, 7, 9, 10, 11, 50
    vs. handheld, 29
Tablesaw extensions, 71–77
Tablesaws, 141
Tabletops, 66, 68, 69–70, 80–81, 82–83
Table workpieces, 158, 160–66
Tapering dovetails, 150–55
Tearout, avoiding
    climb/push cutting and, 131–32, 133
    on moldings, 139–41, 142–44
    template-routing and, 61, 100, 118, 121
    See also Grain of wood
Template routing (pattern routing), 60–61, 116–21
    bandsaws for, 95, 98–100, 120
    bits for, 38, 94–95, 100, 120
    for curved designs, 94–95
    cutting and sanding, 117, 119–20

    jigs for, 38–39, 98–100, 127
    materials for, 116
    pin guides for, 68
    procedure for, 120–22
    troubleshooting, 119
    wood grain and, 60–61, 100, 118, 121
Templates, 116–21
    curves with, 137
    decorative cuts and designs with, 126–27
    for guide bushings, 124–30
    making, 116–20
    multiples with, 39, 60, 127
    pattern-routing jigs for, 39
    piercing, 126
    problems with, 121
    for router plates, 73
    for shelf-pin holes, 127, 128
    using, 120–21
    See also Jigs; Template routing
Tenons
    cutting, 29, 55
    flush-trimming, 44
    See also Mortises, cutting; Rabbets
Trammels, 129
Trend routers, 18
Trim routers, 12–19
    features, compared, 12, 14, 19
    manufacturers, compared, 15–18
    usefulness/versatility of, 6, 7, 8, 10, 12, 13
Triton
    plunge routers, 21, 23, 27
    table routers, 9, 74, 76
Turning jigs, 111–12

U
Ultrahigh molecular weight (UHMW) plastic, 113, 115

V
Vacuums, 68, 69, 72, 74, 76, 77
    See also Dust collection
Veneers, 103–4, 133, 136

W
Wood grain. *See* Grain of wood

Z
Zero-clearance fences, 101, 102, 103, 139–40

If you like this book, you'll love *Fine Woodworking.*

Read *Fine Woodworking* Magazine:

Get seven issues, including our annual *Tools & Shops* issue, plus FREE iPad digital access. Packed with trusted expertise, every issue helps build your skills as you build beautiful, enduring projects.

Subscribe today at:
FineWoodworking.com/4Sub

Discover our *Fine Woodworking* Online Store:

It's your destination for premium resources from America's best craftsmen: how-to books, DVDs, project plans, special interest publications, and more.

Visit today at:
FineWoodworking.com/4More

Get our FREE *Fine Woodworking* eNewsletter:

Improve your skills, find new project ideas, and enjoy free tips and advice from Fine Woodworking editors.

Sign up, it's free:
FineWoodworking.com/4Newsletter

Become a FineWoodworking.com member

Join to enjoy unlimited access to premium content and exclusive benefits, including: 1,400 in-depth articles, over 400 videos from top experts, monthly giveaways, contests, special offers, and more.

Discover more information online:
FineWoodworking.com/4Join